INTERMEDIATE CERTIFICATE

MUSICIANSHIP

VINCENT CLEARY

FOLENS

Acknowledgements

Folens wish to thank the following for permission to use visual material in this book: Eric Auerbach FRPS (Stravinsky conducts; Musical Instruments and Players), Ronald Sheridan's Photo Library (The Parthenon), Houston Rogers Collection, Theatre Museum, Victoria and Albert Museum (Scene from Carmen).

"Bach advises an organ builder" is reproduced from Ladybird book "Lives of the Great Composers Book 1", with the permissions of the publishers, Ladybird Books Ltd., Loughborough, England.

We wish to thank also the various other publishers, Museums, Galleries, *etc.* as credited in the text.

While every effort has been made to reach copyright holders, we have failed to contact some. If any of these latter wish to contact us we would be pleased to come to some arrangement with them.

Setting by Folens Publishers

Printed at the press of the publisher

Edited by Mary Buggle, Folens Publishers.

ISBN
0 86121 176 6
90 9 8 7 6 5 4 83

FOREWORD

This book presents in one volume the material required for the *Intermediate Music and Musicianship Programme.*

The prescribed songs are printed in full with background information. A recording of the songs, in cassette form, made by Young Irish Singers under the direction of Professor Paul Deegan, is available from the Publishers.

The orchestral works are treated in a series of analytical notes and a continuous melodic outline of the works is given. Instrumental cues and expression marks are included to help students follow the music and as a step towards score-reading.

The sections on theory and history are planned to enable teachers to adopt their own individual approaches to the course. The treatment is broad in the hope that students will discover areas of particular interest and thereby make their introduction to music a lasting and enjoyable experience.

As listening to music is an important aspect of the Musicianship Programme, aural exercises are included in the Appendix. These are designed to promote closer and more critical listening. They are suggestions only, from which further questions may be formulated. The Exercise material includes the main themes from the prescribed works and songs, in random order. These may be found helpful in promoting aural and visual familiarity with the course material. Staves are supplied throughout the text on which students may copy down excerpts from the songs and works. Questions based on the preceding pages are also interspersed throughout the text for revision purposes. Hopefully, the index will enable students to carry out independent project work.

Abbreviations used in the Orchestral section:

Orchestra	*Orc*	Cello	*Vc*	Clarinet	*Clar*
Full orchestra	*Tutti*	Bass	*DB*	Bassoon	*Bass*
Strings	*Str*	Woodwind	*WW*	Continuo (Bach)	*C*
Violin	*Vln*	Flute	*Fl*	Solo Trumpet	
Viola	*Vla*	Oboe	*Ob*	(Haydn)	*S*

Contents

Chapter 2 — Orchestral Scores. 57

Excerpts From:

1 — Songs

Veni Creator

From the earliest days of christianity music played an important part in religious services. Sacred airs were taught by one generation to the next. Attempts were often made to write down music and around 900 AD staff notation became established. From then on church music, known as *Plainsong* or *Gregorian Chant,* was notated on the four-line stave. Airs like *Veni Creator* are examples of the earliest known music of any kind, and may well be seventeen hundred years old, or more. As Plainsong was said to be the music of the angels, great trouble was taken to preserve it; changes or additions were jealously rejected. Unlike folk music, Plainsong airs have not changed with the passage of time.

Plainsong has neither time-signature nor bar lines because there is no regular beat; the rhythm is taken from the latin words. Usually the melodies are modal. Some features of Plainsong notation are:

The **C** clef is used here. (The third line is **C**.)
All notes are of equal length.
Accent slightly the first note of a group.
Accent slightly notes with a stroke underneath.
The final notes of each of each phrase are softened and sustained.
The dotted note is a lengthened note.

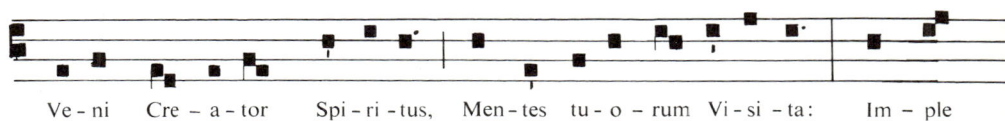

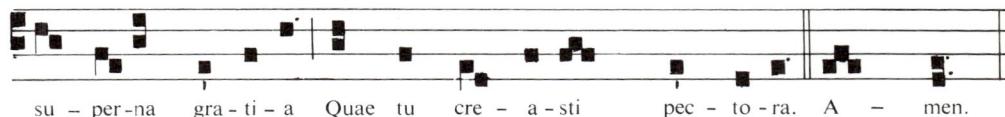

Ve - ni   Cre - a - tor   Spi - ri -tus,   Men - tes   tu - o - rum   Vi - si - ta :   Im — ple

su — per -na   gra - ti – a   Quae   tu   cre - a - sti   pec - to - ra.   A — men.

2   Accende lumen sensibus,
      Infunde amorem cordibus,
      Infirma nostri corporis
      Virtute firmans perpeti.

3   Hostem repellas longius,
      Pacem que dones protinus;
      Ductore sic te praevio,
      Vitemus omne noxium.

1   Come Holy Ghost our souls inspire,
     And lighten with celestial fire;
     Thou the anointing Spirit art,
     Who dost Thy sevenfold gifts impart.

2   Thy blessed unction from above
     Is comfort, life, and fire of love;
     Enable us with perpetual light
     The dullness of our blinded sight.

3   Anoint and cheer our soiled face
     With the abundance of Thy grace:
     Keep far our foes, give peace at home;
     Where Thou art guide, no ill can come.

Exercise

Write down the melody of *Veni Creator* in modern notation.

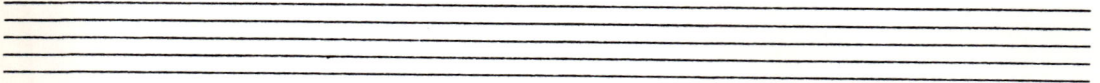

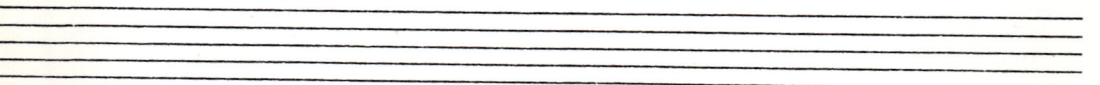

Bearing High the Sacred Cross

Tradition claims that this air was sung by the Crusaders on entering Jerusalem in 1099 under Godfrey de Bouillon. The words, written later, include the Crusaders' war-cry, *It is the Will of God*. The air was used as a hymn in the Middle Ages.

The loose form and the simple metre show its debt to Plainsong. Secular music grew beside religious music, but secular music gradually discarded the modes for the familiar major and minor keys, and also adopted the stricter rhythm of the dance.

Largo

Bear — ing high the sac – red Cross 'Gainst the

foe, Fear — ing nei — ther pain nor strife,

Free — ly off – 'ring limb and life,

'Tis the "Will of God", we know!

In His name we on – ward go.

2 Come from far o'er hill and dale,
    Flood and field,
Armed and mounted, squire and knight
Bear the Cross on helmet bright,
Blazoned banner, shoulder, shield,
Ne'er to foe to bend or yield.

3 Come and see Jerusalem,
    Glorious sight!
Winged each heart, and winged each heel;
Braced each arm with trusty steel;
Valiantly for God to fight,
'Tis His will! His holy Right!

4 Now a thousand voices cry
    Glad and free,
"Hail Jerusalem! all hail!
Theme of minstrel, pilgrim-tale;
Scene of blessed Calvary
And the holy Passion Tree!"

5 Lead the charge with courage bold,
    Wounds contemn!
Still to conquest pressing on
Now the victory is won!
Christian Godfrey we acclaim,
"Conqu'ror of Jerusalem!"

In Dulci Jubilo

This song can be traced to the fourteenth century as a cradle song in a Christmas Mystery play. 'Secular' hymns like this gradually replaced latin Plainsong in German liturgy, although this was against the rules of the Church. Local language and 'folk' masses were heard in Germany long before the Reformation. Luther felt that people should be helped to understand the mass. A skilled musician himself, one of his 'offences' was to promote congregational singing. Bach, who was a Lutheran, continued the work of adapting secular music for church use; he used this song as a chorale and also arranged it as an organ piece.

The use of two languages (macaronic poetry) in poetry is seen where one language is giving way to another, e.g. when latin was giving way to local languages. In Ireland some poetry was written with a mixture of Irish and English lines. Often, the Irish lines concealed a veiled message or a humourous comment on the English lines.

The uncomplicated, little accented style of these songs shows their relationship to Plainsong. They were very suitable for learning and singing by a crowd of people. Many hymns of this kind were originally used in the Catholic Church; after the Reformation they were banned; but now they are again reinstated in Catholic liturgy.

2 O Jesu parvule,
    For thee I long alway;
    Comfort my heart's blindness,
    O puer optime,
    With all thy loving kindness,
    O princeps gloriae.
    Trahe me post te!
    Trahe me post te!

3 O Patris caritas!
    O Nati lenitas!
        Deeply were we stained
    Per nostra crimina;
        But thou for us hast gained
    Coelorum gaudia.
    O that we were there!

4 Ubi sunt gaudia
    In any place but there?
        There are angels singing
    Nova cantica,
        And there the bells are ringing
    In Regis curia.
    O that we were there!

Glossary

In dulce jubilo — in sweet jubilation
In praesehio — in a manger
Matris in gremino — in his mother's lap
Alpha es et O — You are the Alpha and the Omega

O Jesu parvule — O tiny Jesus
O puer optime — O best child
O princeps gloriae — O prince of glory
Trahe me post te — Draw me after you

O Patris caritas — O love of the Father
O Nati lenitas — O gentleness of the Son
Per nostra crimina — Through our crimes
Coelorum gaudia — The joys of the heavens

Ubi sunt — Where are joys
Nova cantica — New songs
In Regis curia — In the court of the King.

O Sacred Head

Air: H.L. Hassler (1564-1612)
Words: St Bernard of Clairvaux?

H.L. Hassler was an important German organist and composer. He composed this air as a love song in 1601 but soon adapted it for use as a church *chorale*. Like other early Luthern hymnal compilers, Hassler, "purified popular art by substituting good fresh spirited texts and words for the ugly material now in use."

The air was used by Bach in his St Matthew Passion, written for Good Friday, 1729 and it is known as the Passion chorale. A heavy-footed modal air, it is very well suited to congregational singing.

2   The Lord of every nation
    Was hung upon a tree;
    His death was our salvation,
    Our sins, His agony.
    O Jesus by Thy Passion,
    Thy life in us increase;
    Thy death for us did fashion
    Our pardon and our peace.

The Wraggle Taggle Gipsies

Somerset air

This song dramatises the story of a young lady who deserts her rich husband to join a gipsy band. In ballad style, the story is told in bare outline. The words of the husband and the wife are given without comment. However sad the story, the mood of the music seems to commend the adventurous spirit of the wife.

Three gip – sies stood at the cas – tle gate, They sang so high, they sang so low, The la – dy sate in her cham – ber late, Her heart it melt – ed a – way as snow.

2   They sang so sweet, they sang so shrill,
That fast her tears began to flow,
And she laid down her silken gown,
Her golden rings and all her show.

3   She plucked off her high heeled shoes,
Amade of Spanish leather, O.
She would in the street, with her bare, bare feet,
All out in the wind and weather, O.

4   "O saddle to me my milk-white steed,
And go and fetch me my pony, O.
That I may ride and seek my bride,
Who is gone with the wraggle taggle gipsies, O."

5 O he rode high and he rode low,
    He rode through wood and copses too,
    Until he came to an open field
    And there he espied his a-lady, O.

6 "What makes you leave you house and land
    Your golden treasures for to go?
    What makes you leave your new-wedded lord,
    To follow the wraggle taggle gipsies, O?"

7 "What care I for my house and land?
    What care I for my treasure, O?
    What care I for my new-wedded lord?
    I'm off with the wraggle taggle gipsies, O!"

8 "Last night you slept on a goose-feather bed,
    With the sheet turned down so bravely, O.
    Tonight you'll sleep in a cold open field,
    Along with the wraggle taggle gipsies, O."

9 "What care I for a goose-feather bed,
    With the sheet turned down so bravely, O?
    Tonight I'll sleep in a cold open field,
    Along with the wraggle taggle gipsies, O."

Richard of Taunton Dean

Somerset air (eighteenth century)

This song has some features in common with the other Somerset air, *The Wraggle Taggle Gipsies*. The story is told in dramatic dialogue. Much of the air is repetitive; Compare the first two bars with the next two. From bar five onwards, a simple figure is used to imitate the trotting of a horse.

Vivace

Last New Year's morn, as I've heard say, Young Rich-ard he mount-ed his dap — ple grey. He trot-ted a-long from Taun-ton Dean To court the par-son's daugh-ter Jean, Sing-ing dum-ble-dum dear-y, dum-ble-dum dear-y, dum-ble-dum dear-y, dum-ble-dum dear-y, dum-ble-dum day.

2 Miss Jean she came without delay,
To hear what Richard had got to say;
"I s'pose that you know me, Mistress Dean,
I'm honest Richard of Taunton Dean." *Singing. . . etc*

3 "I'm honest though I be but poor,
I never was in love before;
My mother bade me come to woo,
And I can fancy none but you," *Singing. . . etc*

4   "Suppose that I should be your bride
     How much for me would you provide?
     For I can neither sew nor spin,
     Pray, what can your day's work bring in?" *Singing. . . etc.*

5   "Why, I can plough, and can sow,
     And to the market I can go
     With Guv'nor Johnson's straw and hay,
     And earn near ninepence every day," *Singing. . . etc.*

6   "Fie ninepence that will never do,
     I must have silks and satins too;
     Ninepence a day won't buy us meat,"
     "Adzooks!" says Dick, "I've a sack of wheat," *Singing. . . etc.*

7   Dick's compliments did so delight,
     They made the family laugh outright;
     Young Richard sighed, no more would say,
     He kicked old Dobbin and rode away. *Singing. . . etc.*

Exercise

 (i) Describe some of the features of early music as seen in the songs you have studied.
(ii) In your own words, tell the story of each of the last two ballads.

Flowers in the Valley

Old English melody

The words of this old ballad with a love theme are given in modern form.

Dolce

O there was a wom-an and she was a wid - ow, Fair are the flowers in the vall - ey, With a daught-er as fair as a fresh sun-ny mead-ow, The Red, the Green and the Yell - ow. The Harp, the Lute, the Pipe, the Flute, the Cym - bal, Sweet goes the treb-le Vi-o - lin. The maid so rare and the flowers so fair, To - ge-ther they grew in the vall - ey.

2   There came a Knight all clothed in red,
      Fair are the flowers in the valley.
    "I would thou wert my bride," he said,
      The Red, the Green and the Yellow.
    The Harp, the Lute, the Pipe, the Flute, the Cymbal,
      Sweet goes the treble Violin.
    "I would," she sighed, "ne'er wins a bride!"
      Fair are the flowers in the valley.

3   There came a Knight all clothed in Green,
       Fair are the flowers in the valley.
   "This maid so sweet might be my queen,"
       The Red, the Green and the Yellow.
   The Harp, the Lute, the Pipe, the Flute, the Cymbal,
       Sweet goes the treble Violin.
   "Might be," sighed she, "will ne'er win me!"
       Fair are the flowers in the valley.

4   There came a Knight, in yellow was he,
       Fair are the flowers in the valley.
   "My bride, my queen, thou must with me!"
       The Red, the Green and the Yellow.
   The Harp, the Lute, the Pipe, the Flute, the Cymbal,
       Sweet goes the treble Violin.
   With blushes red, "I come", she said;
       "Farewell to the flowers of the valley."

Exercise

Make a list of scme of the features usually found in ballads. Consider both words and music.

The Mermaid

This rousing ballad of the sea recalls the superstition that a mermaid was an omen of disaster. A poetic ballad often tells of sad events in cheerful terms. So the spirited mood of this air is in keeping with the mood of the poem, even though the events are tragic.

Moderato

One Fri – day morn when we set sail, And our ship not far from land, We there did es – py a fair pret-ty maid,With a comb and a glass in her hand, her hand, her hand,With a comb and a glass in her hand. While the ra – ging seas did roar, And the storm-y winds did blow, And we jol-ly sail-or boys were up, up a-loft, And the land-lubb-ers ly – ing down be-low, be-low, be-low,And the land-lubb-ers ly – ing down be – low.

2   Then up spoke the captain of our gallant ship,
        Who at once our peril did see,
    "I have married a wife in fair London town,
        And this night she a widow will be." *For the raging seas. . . etc.*

3   And then up spoke the little cabin boy,
        And a fair hair'd boy was he;
    "I've a father and a mother in fair Portsmouth town,
        And this night they will weep for me." *For the raging seas. . . etc.*

4   Then three times round went our gallent ship,
        And three times round went she;
    For the want of a lifeboat they both went down,
        As she sunk to the bottom of the sea. *For the raging seas. . . etc.*

The Arethusa

Music: William Shield (1748 — 1829)
Words: Prince Hoare

Although once very popular, little of Shield's work is now known. *The Arethusa* is a 'composed' ballad with the fault that it lacks both the freshness of folk song, and the ingenuity of art-song.

The background of the song is interesting. The American War of Independence had just begun. France and Spain had sided with the rebellious British colonies, who were led by Benjamin Franklin. On June 17th, 1778, the twenty-eight gun British ship, *Arethusa,* was challenged in the English Channel by the thirty gun *Belle Poule* of France. After a fight of five hours, during which the British lost forty-four men and the French forty-five, the *Belle Poule* ran to safety. It was a hollow victory for Britain, but at a time when the morale of the British navy was low, this song endeavoured to restore confidence. The songwriter exaggerates the British victory — an early example of war propaganda.

The melody is rather ornamental, in five free phrases. The last phrase, is a composite of the first two phrases.

Alla Marcia

Come all ye jol - ly sail - ors bold, Whose hearts are cast in hon - our's mould, While Eng - lish glo - ry I un - fold. Hur - rah for the A - re - thu - sa! She is a fri - gate tight and brave As ev - er stemmed the roll - ing wave; Her men are staunch to their fav' - rite launch; And when the foe shall meet our fire, Soon - er than strike we'll all ex - pire On board of the A - re - thu - sa!

2 'Twas with the Spring fleet she came out,
The English Channel to cruise about,
When four French sail in show so stout,
Bore down on the Arethusa.
The famed Belle Poole straight ahead did lie,
The Arethusa seemed to fly,
Not a sheet or a tack or a brace did she slack
Though the Frenchmen laughed and thought it stuff;
But they knew not a handful of men so tough
On board the Arethusa.

3 The fight was off the Frenchman's land,
We drove them back upon their strand,
For we fought till not a sail would stand,
Of the gallant Arethusa.
And now we've driven the foe ashore,
Never to fight with Britons more,
Let each fill a glass to his fav'rite lass,
A health to our Captain and officers true,
And all that fought hard in that jovial crew
On board the Arethusa.

Art Thou Troubled?

Music: Handel, (1685 – 1759)
Words: W.G. Rothery

As a young man, Handel visited Italy and discovered a new kind of opera there. Later he settled in London and wrote many 'Italian' operas. *Art Thou Troubled?* is an aria from the opera *Rodelinda* which he produced in 1725. It is a good example of the *Da Capo* aria, some features of which are:

A: Prelude; vocal section and interlude.
B: A vocal section in contrasting keys.
A: A direct repeat of the first section (A)

Sonata form is, to some degree, an enlarged version of the *Da Capo* aria. As Italian audiences were more interested in the music than in the story of an opera they did not mind listening to a repeat. The singer, however, usually showed his skill by varying the repeated section with impromptu ornaments. It is not surprising to hear Italian opera sometimes described as a concert in fancy dress. Indeed, it was customary for an opera singer to take a bow, and leave the stage after a well-received aria. Even to the present the emphasis in Italian opera is on the music rather than the story.

The English words of the aria bear no relation to the original, but the mood is similar. In the opera, Bernarido, the King of Lombardy, sings the aria among the tombs of his ancestors while longing for the return of his wife, Rodelinda. It was a convention of Italian opera to have a lady play the leading male role; although sung by a king, Handel did intend this aria for a contralto voice.

The quiet melody rises to a confidant climax. The first question and its answer is a miniature of the whole song. The second question 'Art thou weary?' is answered by phrases of varying length.

source of all glad – ness, heals thy sad – ness. At her

shrine, Mu – sic, mu – sic, ev – er di – vine,

Mu – sic, mu – sic call – eth, With voice di –

vine.

When the wel-come spring is smil-ing, All the earth with flow'rs be –

guil – ing, Af-ter win-ter's drear-y reign, Sweet-est mu – sic doth at – tend her, Heav'n-ly

har-mon-ies doth lend her, Chant-ing prais-es in her train, chant-ing prais-es in her train.

Exercise

(i) What points of difference do you find between *Art Thou Troubled* and *Richard of Taunton Dean*?

(ii) Find out more about the life of Handel.

Where the Bee Sucks

Music: Thomas A. Arne, (1710 — 1778)
Words: Shakespeare, (1550 — 1616)

T.A. Arne was the most important musician of his time in England. He composed many songs and operas and wrote incidental music for plays. He lived for two years in Dublin. His larger works are not heard nowadays, but many of his arias and songs are well known.

This song is part of the incidental music which he wrote for *The Tempest* in 1746. It is sung by the perky spirit, Ariel, who has just been promised freedom by his master, Prospero. Because Ariel is a light-hearted slave, the music has a whimsical character; the accompaniment playfully imitates the owl's call, and the melody behaves like a butterfly on the words 'Merrily, merrily. . .' The words of the song differ slightly from Shakespeare's.

The opening figure which is heard several times is a unifying factor in the melody. After four bars the melody modulates to the dominant, and only returns to the tonic in the second vocal section.

mer-ri-ly, af – ter sun-set mer-ri – ly:

Mer-ri – ly, mer-ri – ly, shall I live

now, Un – der the blos-som that hangs on the bough, Mer-ri – ly,

mer – ri – ly, shall I live now, Un – der the blos-som that hangs on the

bough, Un-der the blos – som that hangs on the bough.

Fine

Exercise

What do you think are the main differences between art songs and ballads?

The Sailor's Song

Music: J. Haydn, (1732–1809)

Haydn was a composer who always moved in the best circles. During his lengthy visits to London he played regularly with the musical members of the royal family. *The Sailor's Song,* which appeared in 1794, shows that he could convey the spirit of the British sailor as well as any English-born composer. It is easy to imagine that he dashed off this song to please a royal friend.

The accompaniment contributes as much as the words by depicting the hazards and the joys of the seafaring life. When not playing a sailor's hornpipe, the accompanist is pretending to be a full-scale orchestra doing impressions of storms, gales and military bands.

Some notable effects are:

(i) dramatic pauses on the words 'war' and 'death', preceded by fanfare effect;

(ii) climax on the words 'Britain's glory';

(iii) the treatment of the words 'hurly burly'.

Exercise

Listen to some other song of the sea or a sea shanty. How does it compare with either
The Sailor's Song or *The Mermaid.*

Rose Among the Heather

Poem: Goethe, (1749–1832)
Music: Schubert, (1779–1828)

Schubert, the greatest songwriter, achieved little fame or success in his lifetime. This song, which he wrote at the age of eighteen, shows his command of melody.

As in a ballad, the same music is used for all verses. This form of art-song is called Strophic. The rhythmic accompaniment is simple but sparkling, and the marked pause in the codetta invites the listeners to join the singer in spirit.

2   Said the youth, I'll call thee now, / Rose, among the heather,
     Said the rose, my thorn, I vow, / Thou shalt feel, 'tis sharp enow,
     Me thou shalt not gather. / Rose thou pretty rose so red,
     Rose among the heather.

3   But the youth impatient cull'd / Rose among the heather,
     Rose stung sharply as he pull'd, / But her days, alas, were told,
     Wounded both together. / Rose, thou pretty rose so red,
     Rose among the heather.

The Trout

English Words: W.G. Rothery
Music: Schubert, (1797–1828)

This well-loved song first appeared when Schubert was twenty years old. Obviously, he too liked the air very much because he revised it many times and also used it in the piano quintet known as, *The Trout*. Schubert, himself, tells how the song nearly came to a sorry end. When he had finished work on it at midnight, he was so exhausted that he emptied the contents of the ink-pot, instead of the sand-box, over his manuscript.

There is a notable 'splashing' figure in the accompaniment which runs right through the first two verses. In the third verse, there is a change of figure to describe the catching of the fish. When the fish is caught, the original air and its accompaniment returns.

Allegretto

stood be-side a brook-let That spark-led on its way, And saw be-neath the
ang-ler there was stand-ing, With rod and line in hand, In — tent up-on the

wave – lets A ti-ny trout at play; As swift-ly as an ar – row He
fish – es, A sport-ive fear – less band; " 'Tis vain,"said I, "good neigh-bour, To

dart-ed to and fro, The gay-est of the fish – es A – mong the reeds be-
fish a brook-let clear, The fish will surely see you Up – on the bank so

low, The gay-est of the fish – es A – mong the reeds be – low.
near, The fish will sure-ly see you Up – on the bank so near.

The lyrics under the music:

2. An
3. But   skil-ful was the
ang — ler   And art — ful   too.   The crys-tal   brook-let's depths de-
fil — ing,   He   hid   the fish from   view;   And   then his skill re - new-ing,   The
fish — es   un - heed-ing took the   bait,   And   I   was left la - ment - ing   My
ti — ny trout - let's   fate,   And   I   was left la - ment-ing My   ti —ny   trout - let's
fate.

Exercise

What are the principal features of an art song?

On Wings of Song

Poem: Heine, (1797–1856)
Music: Mendelssohn, (1809–1847)

This evergreen song was composed by Mendelssohn in 1834, early in his short but frantically busy career. The theme of the poem, a common one at that time, is about escape from reality to a paradise of flowers, beach and music. Package holidays not being available then, the escape happens through the agency of the narcotic lotus-flower.

This is a calm melody with a semiquaver accompaniment which has a soporific effect. The rippling accompaniment falters only once, to underline the word 'lotus-flower.' The first two verses use the same melody and the third verse is a shortened form of it. There is a vocal coda which fades out on the mediant, the accompaniment being left to dissolve the vision. An individual touch of Mendelssohn's is the way in which he concludes without slackening the pace. The arrangement of the phrases is worth studying as is the use of downwards leaps.

balm – y lo – tus flower.
on the breeze it swells.
2. The
3. And there we will sit and
rest us, Un-der the palm tree's shade And dream that love has
bless'd us, And joy will nev – er fade, That
joy will nev — er fade,
nev — er fade.
pp
Fine

Two Eyes of Brown

Words: H.C. Anderson, (1805–1875)
Music: E. Greig, (1843–1907)

This song is from a group called *Melodies of the Heart,* composed in 1864 when Greig was living in Copenhagen (he was from Bergen, in Norway). His two years there were among the happiest of his life. He was a friend of Hans Christian Anderson, the poet and writer of fairy tales, and he set many of Anderson's poems to music. While in Denmark Greig became engaged to Nina Hagerup, a cousin who was also from Bergen, Norway. She was Norway's most notable singer and he wrote this song for her. In 1867 she married Greig and their life together became one of the great love stories of history.

The gentle rocking movement of the accompaniment sets the mood of this song. The tonality is mainly G major but midway through, key and rhythm change with a rather mysterious effect. There is a vocal coda which finishes on the dominant.

Scots Wae Hae

Air: Traditional scottish
Poem: Robert Burns, (1759–1796)

Glossary:
Wha hae wi. . . . . who have with
lour. . . . . approach

Robert Burns, Scotland's most important poet, wrote poems in dialect to match recently-collected traditional airs. One of his frequent themes was the political struggle between England and Scotland. *Scots Wae Hae* recalls the wars of the thirteenth century between Scotland's William Wallace and Robert Bruce, against Edward II of England. The battle referred to is Bannockburn, 1314, when the Scots well and truly trounced the English forces.

The persistant dotted rhythm and the many repeated notes suggest the spirit of determination which brought victory to the Scots. Short two-bar units add to this mood. The form of the air is irregular and is in the *soh* mode. It is well suited to the bagpipes.

2   Wha would be a traitor knave?
    Wha would fill a coward's grave?
    Wha sae base as be a slave?
    Let him turn an' flee!
    Wha, for Scotland's king an' law,
    Freedom's sword would strongly draw,
    Freeman stand and freeman fa',
    Let him on wi' me!

3   By oppression's woes an' pains,
    By your sons in servile chains,
    We will drain our dearest veins,
    But they shall be free.
    Lay the proud usurpers low!
    Tyrants fall in every foe!
    Liberty's in every blow!
    Let us do or dee!

Wi' a Hundred Pipers

Air: Scottish traditional
Poem: Lady Nairne, (1766–1845)

Like Robert Burns, Lady Nairne composed patriotic poetry to match traditional Scottish airs. This song tells a fanciful story of how a hundred pipers under Bonnie Prince Charlie helped to rout a great force of English soldiers. The vigorous melody in compound time uses many leaps, which are mainly based on the primary chords. All the cadences have repeated notes. It is a typical bagpipe air.

2   Oh! our sodger lads look'd braw, look'd braw,
     Wi' their tartans, Kilts an' a', an' a',
     Wi' their bonnets, an' feathers, an' glitt'ring gear,
     An' piobrochs sounding sweet an' clear.
     Will they a' return to their ain dear glen?
     Will they a' return – our Hieland men?
     Second-sighted Sandy look'd fu' wae,
     And mothers grat when they march'd awa'. *Wi' a hundred. . . etc.*

3   Oh wha is foremaist o' a', o' a'?
     Oh wha does follow the blaw, the blaw?
     Bonnie Charlie, the king o' us a', harra!
     Wi' his hundred pipers an' a', an' a'!
     His bonnet an' feather he's wavin' high!
     His prancing steed maist seems to fly!
     The nor' wind plays wi' his curly hair,
     While the pipers blaw in an unco flare!   *Wi a hundred. . . etc.*

4   The Esk was swollen, sae red, sae deep;
     But shouter to shouter the brave lads keep;
     Twa thousand swam ower to fell English ground,
     An' danc'd themselves dry to the piobroch's sound.
     Dumbfounder'd, the English saw, they saw!
     Dumfounder'd, they heard the blaw, the blaw!
     Dumfounder'd, they ran awa', awa'
     Frae the hundred pipers an' a', an' a'!   *Wi' a hundred. . . etc.*

Glossary

Verse 1
an' a'...................... and all
gie 'em a blaw....... give them a blow
Wi' its yetts........... with its gates
ha' .... hall

Verse 2
look'd braw............ looked brave
look'd fu' wae........ looked full of woe
grat.......................... wept

Verse 3
maist .... almost
unco flare.............. uncommon spirit

Verse 4
fell............................ evil

Bonnie Charlie's Noo Awa

Air: Attributed to Neil Gow, (1795–1823)
Poem: Lady Nairne, (1766–1845)

In the times when the majority of people could neither read or write, songs played a big part in communicating and forming political views. It has been said that songs were the history books of the people and that sometimes songs made history. Many songs were composed to encourage and commemorate the efforts of the Catholic Stuart family to regain the throne of Scotland and England, lost to them by James at the battle of the Boyne, 1691. These songs are known as Jacobite songs.

High hopes of success were raised by the return of Charles Edward, fondly known as Bonnie Prince Charlie, in 1745. His inevitable failure provided material for countless patriotic ballads. *Bonnie Charlie's Noo Awa* is one of the best known. Songs like this helped to keep alive the spirit of nationalism in Scotland as did the songs of Thomas Davis and others in nineteenth-century Ireland.

Neil Gow was a member of an Edinburgh family of musicians and music publishers. The air falls into emphatic two-bar units. It uses the pentatonic scale (d, r, m, s, l) *c.f. Ye Banks and Braes,* and *Loch Lomond.*

2   Ye trusted in your Hieland men,
    They trusted you, dear Charlie!
    They kent your hiding in the glen,
    Death and exile braving. *Chorus*

3   English bribes were a' in vain,
    Tho' puir and puirer we mann be;
    Siller canna buy the heart
    That aye beats warm for thine and thee. *Chorus*

4   We watched thee in the gloamin' hour,
    We watched thee in the mornin' grey,
    Though thirty thousand pounds they gie,
    Oh, there is nane that wad betray! *Chorus*

5   Sweet's the laverock's note, and lang,
    Liltin' wildly up the glen;
    But aya to me he sings ae sang,
    "Will ye no come back again?" *Chorus*

Glossary

kent .... knew
siller............. silver
laverock .... lark

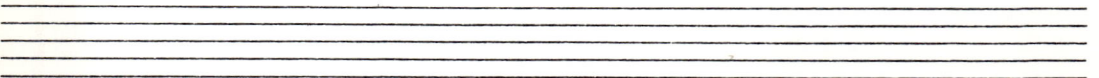

Let Erin Remember

Air: Traditional Irish
Poem: Thomas Moore, (1779–1852)

Like the Scottish poet Robert Burns, Moore wrote poems to match recently-collected native airs. The source of most of his melodies was the collection of Edward Bunting, *Legends of Ancient Ireland* which provided themes for many of Moore's poems. This one pictures prehistoric Ireland. The towers mentioned in the second verse recall the story that Lough Neagh was formed from a magic spring which drowned the entire countryside and its inhabitants.

The melody has a stirring march tune which moves mostly by steps. The dotted rhythm and the full cadences at each phrase ending have a forceful effect.

Let E-rin re-mem-ber the days of old 'Ere her faith – less sons be-tray'd her; When Mal – a – chi wore the col-lar of gold, Which he won from the proud in – vad – er; When her Kings, with stand-ards of green un – furl'd, Led the Red Branch Knights to dan – ger, Ere the em' – rald gem of the west-ern world Was set in the crown of a stran – ger.

On Lough Neagh's bank as the fisherman strays,
When the clear cold eve's declining,
He sees the round tow'rs of other days
In the wave beneath him shining;
Thus shall memory often, in dreams sublime,
Catch a glimpse of the days that are over;
Thus sighing, look through the waves of time
For the long faded glories they cover.

Baby Brother Mine

Hungarian melody
English words: W.G. Rothery

There is clear contrast in this melody. The first eight-bar phrase has a step by step movement, while the rest of the melody has a chordal structure and a more varied rhythm.

Andante

Ba – by bro-ther small, With laugh-ing eyes of blue, When you are old and tall, What ev - er shall I do? I've spent such hap-py hours Teach-ing you walk-ing, You have learnt from me All you know of talk – ing.

2 Baby brother mine,
     With pretty golden curls,
   Perhaps when you are nine
     You won't think much of girls,
   But we will ever be
     True to each other,
   You will be to me
     Just my great big brother.

3 When a man you grow,
     And sail away to sea,
   You must, before you go,
     Find room on board for me;
   I'd keep your buttons bright,
     See to your sewing,
   Hold your hand so tight
     When all the winds were blowing.

Battle-hymn of the Republic

Air: W. Steffe?
Poem: J.W. Howe, (1819–1910)

The original words of this song, 'John Brown's body lies a-mouldering in the grave. . . . But his soul goes marching on,' refer to the efforts of John Brown to obtain freedom for negro slaves in America early in the last century. That song became popular during the American Civil War (1861–1865). As a rallying song, it helped to secure the success of Abraham Lincoln and eventually the abolition of slavery. It was a song which helped to make history.

Many poets, including Julia Ward Howe, wrote more sophisticated words for this air. Her version has become a national hymn of the United States. These words, with their biblical flavour, illustrate the self-righteous attitude of all warring people – that God is on their side.

The dotted rhythm produces the same resolute feeling which is found in *Scots Wae Hae.* An examination of the melody will show that all its ideas are contained in the first four-bar phrase. Each two-bar unit ends on a note of the tonic chord; this gives a feeling of completeness and conviction to each statement – just like a slogan. An air which becomes a rallying song usually has this quality.

Pomposo

Mine eyes have seen the glo–ry of the com–ing of the Lord: He is

tramp-ling out the vin-tage where the grapes of wrath are stor'd, He hath

loos'd the fate-ful light-ning with His ter-ri-ble swift sword, His truth is march-ing

on. Glo – ry, Glo – ry, Hal – le – lu – jah!

Glo — ry, Glo-ry, Hal-le — lu — jah!   Glo — ry, Glo-ry, Hal-le —

lu — jah, His   truth   is   march — ing   on.

2   I have seen Him in the watchfires of a hundred circling camps;
    They have builded Him an altar in the evening dews and damps;
    I can read the righteous sentence by the dim and flaring lamps,
        His day is marching on. *Chorus*

3   I have read a fiery gospel, writ in burnish'd rows of steel;
    As ye deal with my contemners so with you My grace shall deal;
    Let the Hero born of woman crush the serpent with His heel
        Since God is marching on. *Chorus*

4   In the beauty of the lilies Christ was born across the sea
    With a glory in his bosom that transfigures you and me;
    As He died to make men holy, let us die to make men free!
        While God is marching on. *Chorus*

5   He has sounded forth the trumpet that shall never call retreat;
    He is sifting out the hearts of men before His judgement seat,
    Oh, be swift my soul to answer Him, be jubilant my feet,
        Our God is marching on. *Chorus*

Exercise

Listen to some other patriotic songs and state the message they convey.

Joshua Fight the Battle of Jericho

Negroes on American slave plantations favoured songs with religious themes, now known as 'negro spirituals.' This one tells how the power of God destroyed the walls of Jericho through Joshua's action of blowing trumpets. The message of many of these spirituals was that God would protect His faithful followers.

[c.f. Joshua, Chapter 6: Then the Lord said to Joshua, "March round the city with all the men of war. . . Seven priests shall each carry a ram's horn trumpet before the Ark. . . When you hear the blare of the trumpets. . . . let all the people give a mighty shout of joy; then the wall of the city will collapse so that. . . .]

Syncopation, which occurs in this song, was a favourite device of the negro folk singer. Early in the twentieth century it became a notable feature of jazz. This air uses the scale E, F, G, A, B, D.

2   Up to the walls of Jericho
        He marched with spear in hand;
     "Go blow them ram's horns," Joshua cried,
        " 'Cos the battle am in my hand!"

3   Then the lam' ram sheep horns 'gin to blow,
        Trumpets begin to blow.
     Joshua commanded the children to shout,
        And the walls came tumbling down.

Táimse im Codladh

Poem: Eoin Rua O Suilleabhán

This song which has an interesting form, has a very wide range (a fourteenth). It is an example of the *Aisling* – a poem in which the poet sees a vision of a beautiful lady who represents Ireland. She fires him with love for Ireland and a desire to fight for freedom.

Largo

Tráth - nói - nín   déa - nach i   gcéin   cois   lea-sa dom,

Táim - se im   chod-ladh 's ná   dúis - tear   mé;   Sea

dhearc-as lem   thaobh   an   spéir - bhean   mhais-ea-mhail,

Táim - se im   chod-ladh 's ná   dúis - tear   mé.   Ba

bha - chall - ach   péar - lach   dréim - reach   barr-(a)-chas A

ca - r(a)n - fholt   craobh - ach ag   teacht   léi ar   baill- i-chrith,'Sí ag

caith - eamh na   saeghad trím   thaobh   a   chea-lag mé,

Táim - se im   chod-ladh 'sná   dúis - tear   mé.

Paraphrase

Late in the evening when I was out near a fairy fort, (I'm sleeping, don't waken me) I saw a beautiful enchanted lady beside me. She had a mass of shining hair. She was shooting arrows through my heart, and they wounded me.

Rise up, my children, (she said) and take up your weapons. Throw every foreign rogue into the river. Even if only a few of you survive, let there be risings in every town from Carrick-on-Suir to the edge of Dingle in the west. Lift up your swords and attack the English.

2 Is éirigí, a chlann, agus gabhaig bhur n-airm chughaibh,
Táimse im chodladh 'sná dúistear mé;
Is leagaigí sa tsrúil gach scrúille Sasanaigh,
Táimse im chodladh 'sná dúistear mé:
Mura mairfeadh ach triúr bíodh clú ins gach bail' agaibh
Ó Charraig na Siúire go ciumhais an Daingin thiar:
Ardaigí bhur lann, tugaig fogha faoi na Sasanaigh,
Táimse im chodladh 'sná dúistear mé.

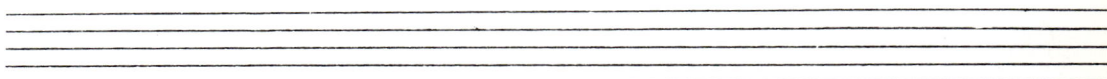

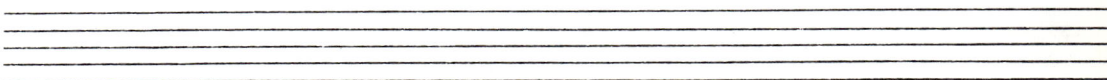

Raithineach, a Bhean Bheag

This is a good-humoured work-song dealing with various tastes in food.

Paraphrase

1   I sent my daughter to Barra na hAoine to get potato cakes or sweet cakes. When she returned home, her father would not taste them. "Rubbish, little woman; Potato cakes with butter on them!"

2   "This bread is not potato cake nor peeled potato. It is made from Spanish flour, brought home in silken bags. The man who eats a cake of it will win the race on the big strand of Aoine."

3   There are fair-headed women in Barra na hAoine, who are not used to making this potato cake. They grind it rough and they leave lumps in the middle of it. Then it puts blisters on the mouth for day and a night.

Allegro

Do   chuir-eas mo ghearr-(a)-chai-le   go   Barr-a   na   hAoin-e   Ag

iarr - aidh staim-pí   nó   cá-caí mil-se, Nuair a   thái-nig sí   a-bhai-le   ní

bhlais-feadh fear an tí   iad,   Is   raith - in - each   a   bhean   bheag,

staim-pí 'gus im air.   Raith-in-each, a bhean bheag, a bhean bheag, a   bhean bheag.

Raith-in -each, a bhean bheag, staim- pí 'gus im air; Raith-in-each, a bhean bheag, a

bhean bheag, a bhean bheag. Raith-in-each, a bhean bheag, is déan-fai-mid an cís- te.

2　Ní staimpí an t-arán seo ná prátaí scríobtha,
Ach plúr ón Spáinn trí áisibh síoda.
An té d'íosfadh císte de ar maidin t'r éis na hoíche,
Do bhuafadh sé an rás ar thrá mhór na hAoine.

3　Ta mná barrfhionna i mBarra na hAoine,
Níl siad taithíoch ar an staimpí seo scríobadh:
Meileann siad garbh é 's bíonn leacacha 'na chroí istigh
's bíonn cloig at a gcarbaid ar feadh lá go h-oíche. Curfá

Seán Ó Dhuibhir

A seventeenth century song from Tipperary of mixed moods, partly of joy in the memory of the chase and partly of bitterness on realising that the days of unrestricted hunting are coming to an end. The compass of the melody is very great.

Paraphrase

When I used to get up on a summer's morning, I heard the sound of the hunt and the sweet music of the birds, badgers and hares, the woodcock with the long beak, and the echos of the heavy guns. The red fox on the rock, horsemen shouting, and a woman on the road, sadly counting her geese. But now the woods are being cut; we must go away. Sean O Dhuibhir of the glens, you are without game.

I am very sad because the shelter is being cut down; the wind from the north is threatening me, and there is death in the sky. My little dog, which used to comfort the children in the bright midday, is tied up and silent. The noble stag is on the rock. If I could get peace for a while, I would go to Galway and leave the land.

Andante

Ar m'éi - rí dom ar mai - din, Grian an tsamh - raidh'g tait – neamh,

Chua - la'n uail á cas-adh, 'Gus ceol binn na n-éan; Broic is míol-ta gearr-a,

Creabhair r a ngob-a fada, Fuaim ag an ma-call-a, Is lámhach gun-naí tréan. An

sionn-ach rua ar an gcarr-aig, Mí-le liú ag marcaigh, Is bean go dubhach san mbealach Ag

áireamh a cuid gé; Ach a - nois tá'n choill á gearradh, Triall-fai-mid thar cal - adh, 'S a

Sheáin Uí Dhuibhir an Ghlean-na, Tá tú gan géim.

2   Is é sin m'uaigineas fada
     Scáth mo chluas á ghearradh,
     An ghaoth aduaidh dom leathadh,
     'Gus bás ins an spéir;
     Mo ghadhairín suairc á cheangal
     Gan cead lúith ná aistíocht',
     A bhainfeadh gruaim den leanabh,
     I meá ghil' an lae.
     Croí na huaisle ar an gcarraig,
     Go ceáfrach buacach beannach,
     A thiocfadh suas ar aiteann,
     Go lá dheireadh'n tsaoil.
     'Sdá bhfaighinnse suaimhneas tamall
     Ó dhaoine uaisle'n bhaile,
     Do thraillfainn féin ar Ghaillimh,
     Is d'fhágfainn an scléip.

Frinseach Thí Róin

This song from the Tuam district was collected around 1890. It tells a hunting story about a local landowner, Christopher ffrench, who had adopted an English title in 1774 and was nicknamed ffrench, Lord of the Seals. The chorus suggests that it was used as a cradle song.

Paraphrase

"Oh!" said the fox, "What shall I do?" Here come the dogs and they will tear me apart. I will be thrown out to suffer the frost, and Frinseach Thí Róin will have my brush in the evening.

Going south through the Hawk Glen, my story is sad; my wind is broken and my tongue is hanging out." The fox was injured going through the bog, and he was destroyed by Frinseach Thi Roin.

Allegretto

"Ó bhó," ars' an sionn - ach, "Cad a dhéan - fas mé féin?

Seo iad na gadhair a - gus stroic – fidh siad mé;

Caith – fear a – mach mé 's beidh an sioc faoi mo shróin, 'S mo

ru – ball tráth – nó – na ag Frin – seach Thí Róin." Rum dum – bel - dum

dum – bel - dum dum – bel - dum dum, Rum dum – bel - dum dum, Rum dum – bel – dum dum, Rum dum – bel – dum dum – bel – dum dum – bel – dum

dum, Cur – mud – geon, Rap – scall – ion, Bí 'do thost, a dhail – tín.

2   '' 'Gabháil anoir ag Gleann Seabhach nár chlaon é mo scéal?
    Bhí m'anáil féin briste 'smo theanga thar mo bhéal'';
    Bascadh an sionnach 'se ag dul trid an móin,
    Mar suaitheadh é'g clampar le Frinseach Thí Róin. *Curfá*

Turas go Tír na nÓg

This is the song of an exile longing to return to Ireland, which he regards as Tír na nÓg. The air is from County Cork.

Paraphrase

The land breeze is blowing and the birds are going to rest. Nature is turning to rest over the fields. From the brown face of the mountain comes the bleating of the lambs, and the sound of the stream is moaning on the strand. There is loneliness in my spirit, and the night feels long. My soul would like to travel with the sun from this sorrow which is in my mind, to a country which will release me from pain.

I am being called from the west by a beautiful voice like a breeze whispering over the bay. I will go to my boat and I pray for a safe crossing. It is not a land of brightness and poetry I seek, but one full of friendliness. Generous hearts dwell in the heart of Ireland. That's where I am going – to Tír na nÓg.

Dolce

Tá gaoth na tír-e'g séid-eadh's tá na héan-laith 'dul chun suain, Tá'n

dubhar ag dul chun sín-eadh ar an mbán, Ó éa-dan rua an

tsléi – bhe tag-ann méil-ea-chán na n-uan, A – gus fuaim na cai-se'g

caoin-eadh ar an trá; Tá uaig – neas ar m'a-nam 's is

fa – da liom an oí – che, Ba mhian lem spio-rad gluais-eacht leis an

ngréin Ón mbuairt seo 'tá ar m'ai – g – ne, is ó chea-l(a)g-rún an

tsaoil, Go tír a bhfaighinn-se fuas-cailt ar mo phéin.

2   Ó, glaotar orm aniar, 'gus is aoibhinn liom an glór,
    Mar bheadh leoithne chaoin ag cogar thar an gcuan;
    Rachad chun mo loinge nó go scaoilfigh mé mo sheol,
    Is go ndeonaítear mo shroicheadh slán anonn.
    Ní tír go n-iomad soilse ná laoithe liom ab fhearr,
    Ach tír bheadh lán de charthanacht im chomhair,
    Mar a maireann féile croíthe idir saoithe Inse Fáil,
    Is ann atá mo thriall, go Tír na nÓg.

An Spéic Seoigheach

A poem from Connaught about a popular figure.

Paraphrase

1 Here comes the Speic Seoigheach escorted by young women and lively men. *Chorus*
2 One morning I was going through the bogs. I met a young girl with her boots in her hand. *Chorus*
3 One fine day I was drinking at the fair of Carra I took a fancy to the daughter of the Big Man. *Chorus*
4 Hither and thither, and always welcome. If I had beer, my love, I would drink your health. *Chorus*

Vivace

Siúd í'n spéic seoigh - each á tóg - áil go hin - tinn-each

Id - in mná óg - a 'gus óg - án - aigh aer - a - cha, 'smo

lil ló a - ba bó. - - - - - - - - - - - - 'Smo ru

lann heigh ru - lann hó ru - lann heigh a hir - i - lann ru -

lann heigh ru - lann a - gus hoch deigh ri deigh ri nann.

2 Bhí mise maidin Mhárta' ag góil trí na Portaithe's casadh cailín óg orm 's a Bróga na hucht aici, 'Smo lil ló aba bó. *Cúrfa*

3 Bhí mé lá aerach ar aonach na Carr' 's mé 'g ól, Thug mé gean éigin d'iníon an bhodaigh mhóir, 's mo lil ló aba bó. *Cúrfa*

4 Siúd ort is diúg ort is naoi gcéad míle fáilte, Dá mbeadh lionn agam, a rú, is mise d'ólfadh do shláinte, is mo lil ló aba bó. *Cúrfa*

Uiseag Bheag Rú

In this Manx song an Irish form of the words is given to show the similarity of the two languages. The scale in which the song is written is G, A, B♭, D, F. It is a gap scale, the fourth and sixth being missing,

English version

1 Little red bird of the black turf-ridge,
   Where did you sleep last night?
   All night long on the briery hedge,
   Rocked by the cruel wind's might.

2 Little red bird of the black turf-ridge,
   Where did you sleep last night?
   All night long on the roof's cold edge,
   Like many a homeless wight.

3 Little red bird of the black turf-ridge,
   Where did you sleep last night?
   All night long on a bush by the bridge,
   Rained on to left and to right.

Allegretto

'Uis - eag   bheag   rú   na   mói — ne   dú,

Mói — ne   dú,   mói — ne   dú,   'Uis - eag   bheag

rú   na   mói — ne   dú,   C'rád   chai — dil   ú

raoir san oí? _ _ _ _ _ _ _ _ _ _ Nach chai – dil mis raoir ar

bár a crao, Bár a crao, bár a

crao, Leis fliag a tuit – eam ar dach tao, Is

och mo chad – la cha tré! _ _ _ _ _ _ _ _ _ _ _ _ _

Irish version

2   'Uiseag bheag rú na móine dú,
     Móine dú, móine dú,
     C'rád chaidil ú raoir san oí?
     Nach chaidil mis raoir ar bár a tonn,
     Br a tonn, Bár a tonn,
     Mar 's ioma mac duine cadla rom,
     Is och! mo chadla cha tré!

3   'Uiseag bheag rú na móine dú,
     Móine dú, móine dú,
     'Uiseag bheag rú na móine dú,
     C'rád chaidil ú raoir san oí?
     Ó, chaidil mis raoir eadar dá dhuilleag,
     Eadar dá dhuilleag, eadar dá dhuilleag,
     Mar cadla an óicean ar cíoch a mhuiming,
     Is ó! mo chadla cha caoin!

Exercise

Mention some features of traditional Irish music. What do you think is meant by *sean nós* singing?

2 —Orchestral Scores

Suite for Orchestra in D major

J.S. Bach

I. Overture

Tpt
cresc.
36
C
Tutti
cresc.
DEVELOPMENT
42
p EPISODE
(Vln)
SUBJECT (Vln)
Ob
p
Tpt
Vla
Vln
Ob
(Tpt)
54
Vla
Vln
p
Tpt
f SUBJECT

Ob + Vln
60
Tpt
cresc.
f
Tutti
66
C
Ob
f
EPISODE
Vln
72
+ Ob
Tutti
Tpt
Ob
SUBJECT
79
Vla
Vln
Ob
Vla
Tpt
Tutti

BRIDGE PASSAGE
Vln
86
RECAPITULATION
Vln + Ob
24
SUBJECT
Vla
C
Tpt
30
Ww + Str
Tpt
Ww + Str
Tutti
cresc.
36
Tpt
C
Tutti
cresc.

II. Air

V. Gigue

Tutti
ff
Ww + Str
Tutti
Ww + Str
13
Tutti
25
Ww + Str
Tutti
Ww + Str
Tutti
Ww + Str
Tutti
Ww + Str
37
Tutti
49
Ww + Str

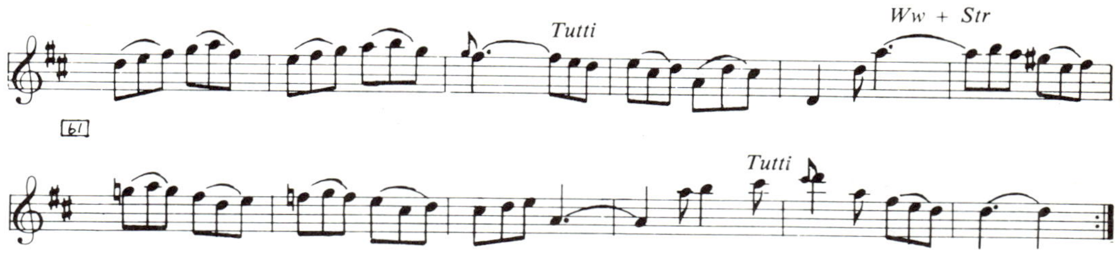

Concerto for Trumpet in E♭ major

Josef Haydn

I.

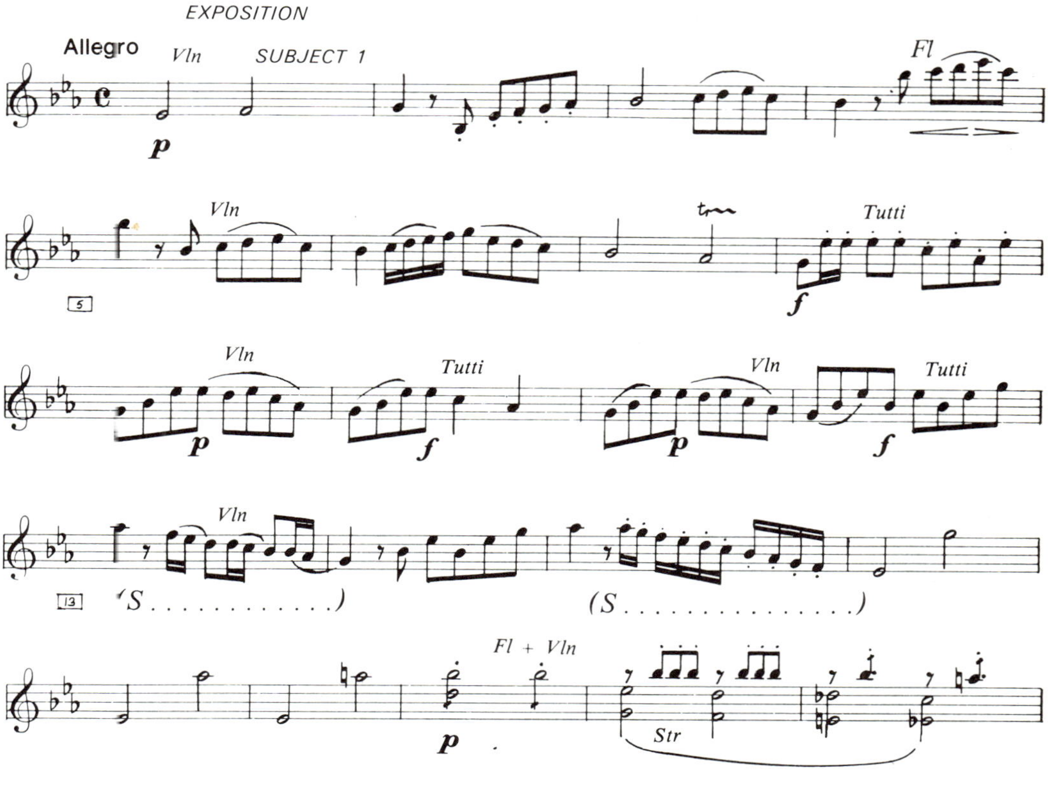

22
Vln
f
+ Ww
Vln
Cresc
29
Ww
Tutti
37
S
f
Fl
p
S
tr
Tutti
45
S
p
Ww
f
S
Tutti
Vln
p
S
f
S
p
53
Vln
S + Vln
Bass
Ww
S

Ww
S
MODULATION TO B♭
(SUBJECT 2)
Vln
Vln
+ Strs
Tutti
Str
S
71
Str
CONCLUSION OF SUBJECT 2
S (CODETTA)
Tutti
Str
79
Ww + Str
ORC. CODETTA
Vln + Ww
Tutti
Fl
88
Vc
DEVELOPMENT [SUBJECT 1 IN C MIN]
S
Vln

97
S
f
Vln
p
(Ww)
105
Vln
114
Str
S
+ Ww
Fl
Tutti (PP)
RECAPITULATION
124
Fl
Tutti
S
p

141
Tutti
f
Ww + Vln
S
p
Vln
f
S
p
149
Vln + Ob
f
S
Vln
156
Vln
p
S
Str
Tutti
f
S
Tutti
Ob
165
Br
(CADENZA)
CODA
Tutti

Quintet for piano and strings in A major
Theme and Variations

Franz Schubert

Theme: Andantino

Strs

Var I

Piano

Var II

Piano

Vla
Vc

DB

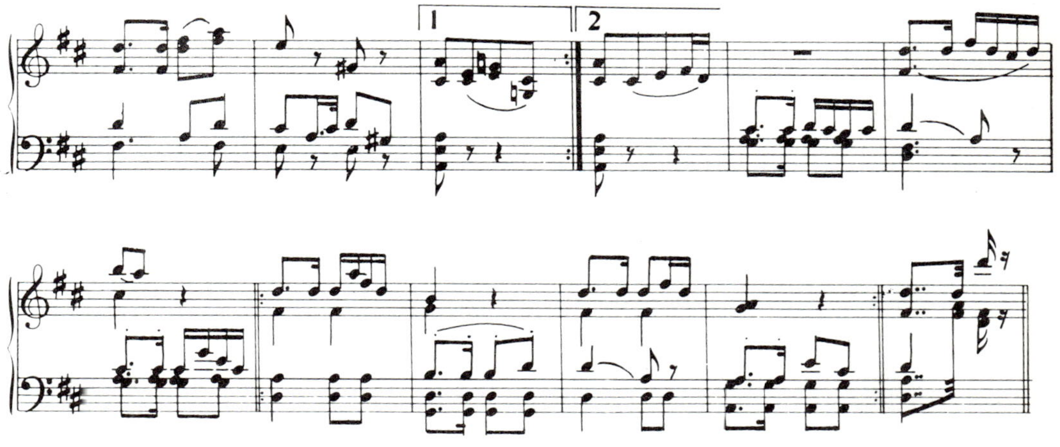

Var. II

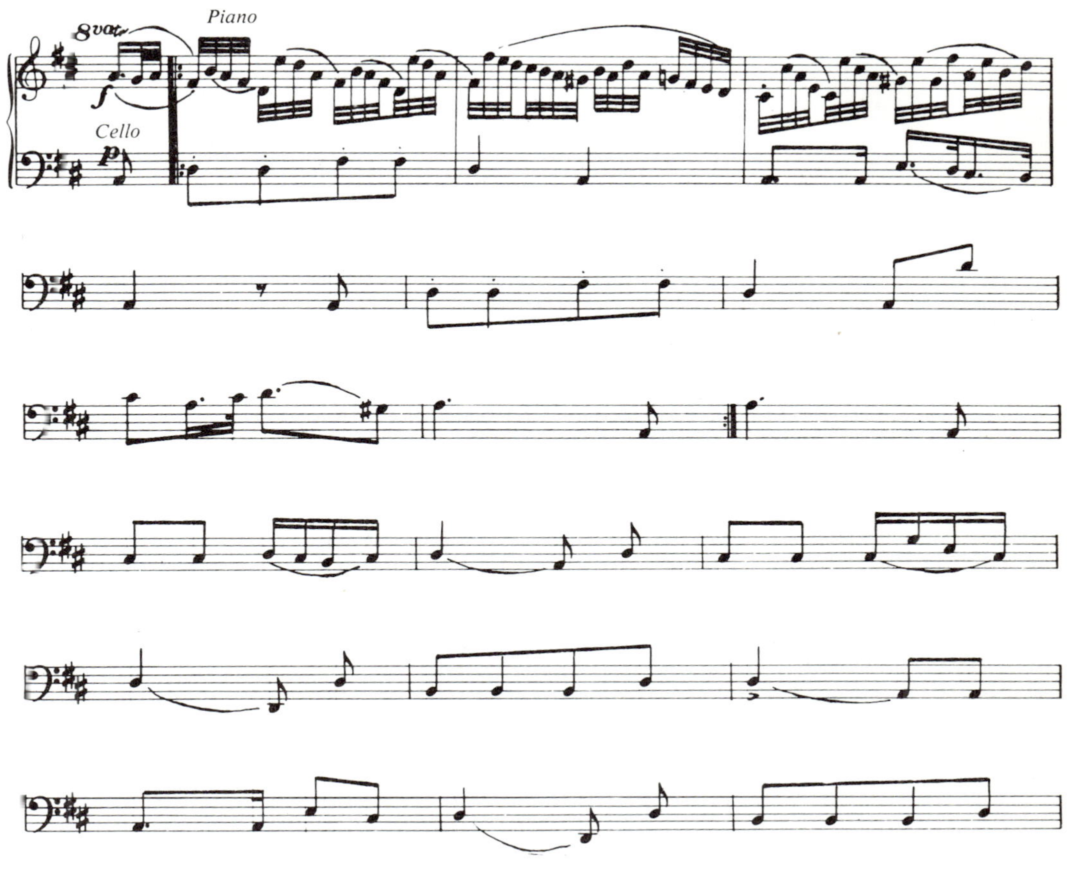

Var. IV

Var. V

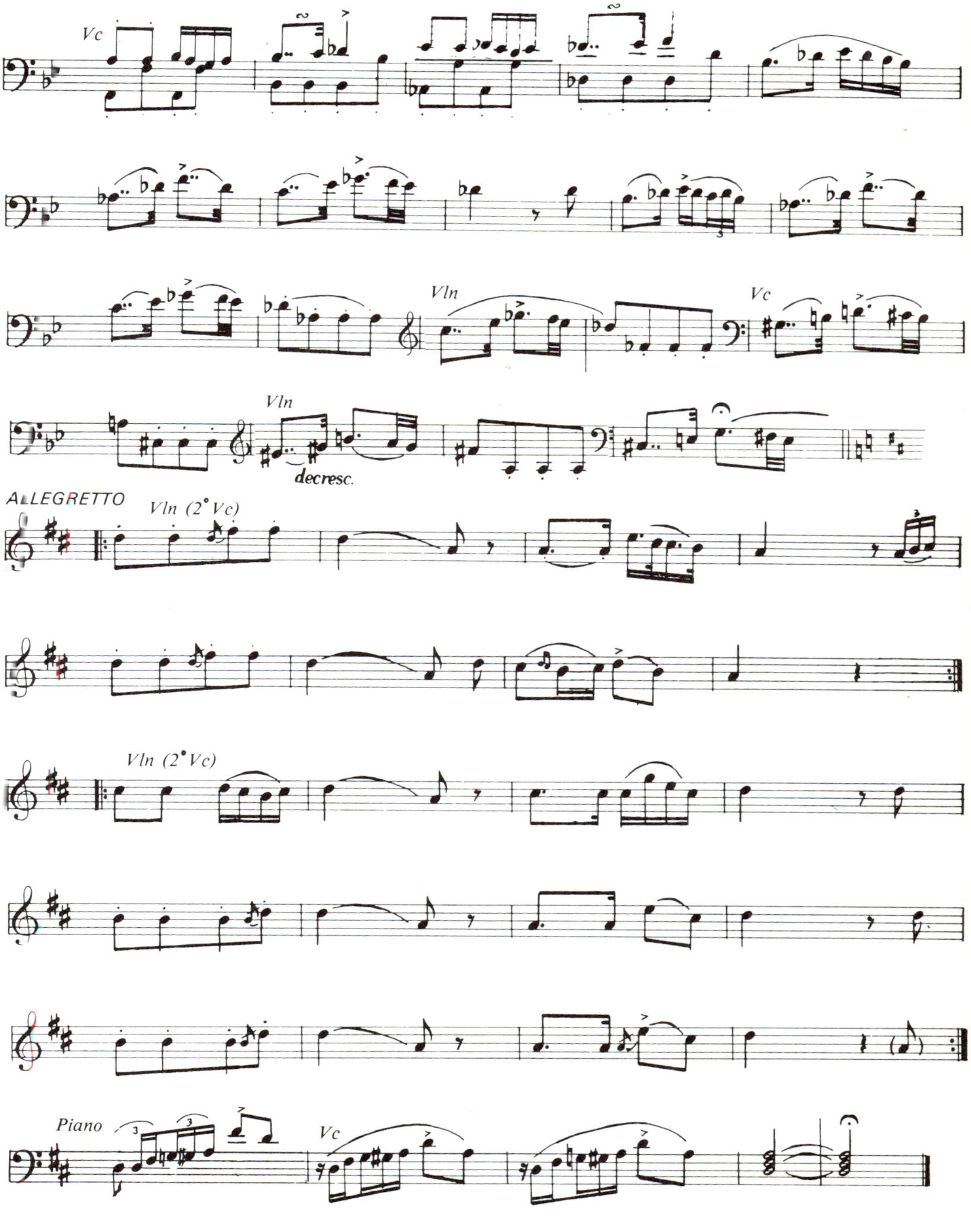
Vc
Vln
Vc
Vln
decresc.
ALLEGRETTO
Vln (2° Vc)
Vln (2° Vc)
Piano
Vc

The Hebrides (Fingal's Cave) Overture

Felix Mendelssohn

Allegro moderato

Vln
Tutti
ff
Vln
p
Clar + Bass
Tutti
42
ff
Vln
pp
Clar + Bass
(Tpt)
Ww
2nd SUBJECT
Bass + Vc
Vln
mf
cresc.
Str
Str
pp
(Fl)
+ Clar
Ob
Clar + Bass
Str
SUBJECT 1
f
ff
Tutti

8va
Str
Ww + Br
87
Ww + Br
Ww
Br
DEVELOPMENT
Str
Ww
Vln
Str
Ww
Str
Clar
Tpt
109
(Fl + Ob)
Clar + Brass
Ww
Tpt
Ww
Hrn
Ww
Clar
Ob + Bass
Tpt
SUBJECT 2
119
decresc.
Vln
Vla

St-
+ Ww
8va
Vln
Fl
cresc.
Vn
138
f
p
Fl
Vln
cresc
14-
f
pp staccato
Ww
Str
Ww
Str
Ww
Str
Ww
Str
Ww
155
cresc.
cresc.
Fl + Clar
f
Ww
163
Str
Clar + Hrn

Ww
Str
8va Tutti
ff
Ww
Fl
Str
Tutti
Fl
Clar + Vln
Vla
Vc
RECAPITULATION
180
p
+ Bass
Vln
Ww
Vln
188
sf
sf
Tutti
sf cresc.
sf
Str
Ob
Vln
Clar SUBJECT 2
198
p
+ Clar 2

(Hrn)
CODA
animato
Ob
8va
Vln
Ww + Br
cresc.
Tutti
Ww
f
226
ff
Vc + DB
Ww
Vln
Ww
Vln
Br
Br
Str
Str
Vc + DB
Vln

Ma Mere l'Oye

(Mother Goose Suite)

Maurice Ravel

I. Pavane de la Belle au bois dormant

(Pavan of the Sleeping Beauty)

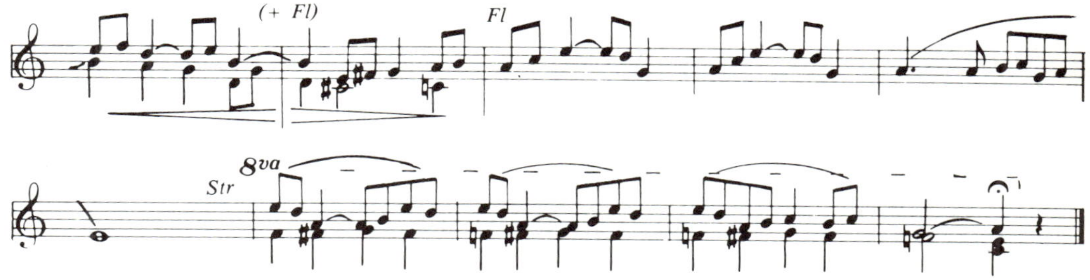

II. Petit Poucet

(Tom Thumb)

Moderato

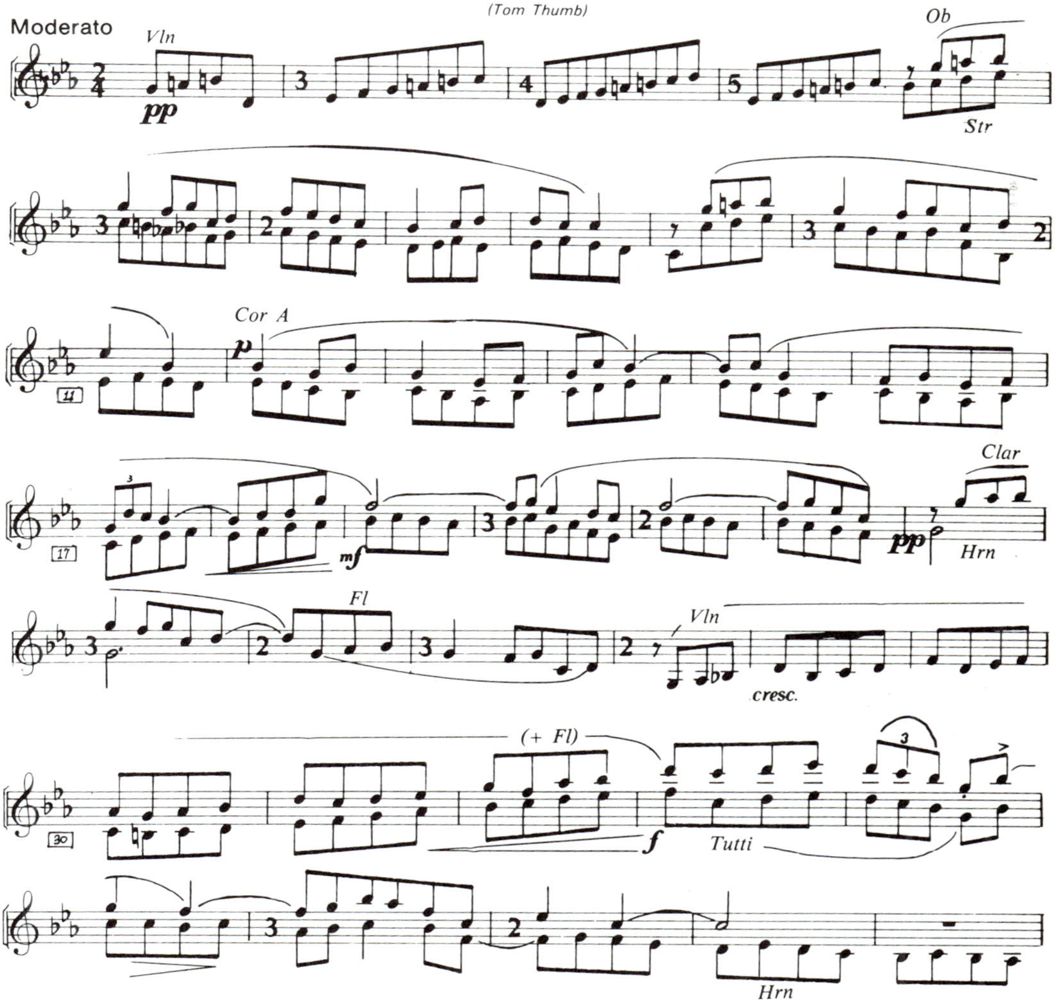

III. Laideronnette, Impératrice des Pagodes

(Laideronnette, Empress of the Pagodes)

Tutti
f
Celesta
mf
p
25
f
p
f
Ww
decresc.
Ob
pp
Strs
Fl
Cor A
43
Fl
Cor A
Fl
Cor A
Fl
Fl + Xylo
+ Celest + Clar
55
cresc
Tutti
ff
2
Fine
1
Ww + Br
f
Fl + Hrn + Harp + Vla
decresc.
Clar
77
pp

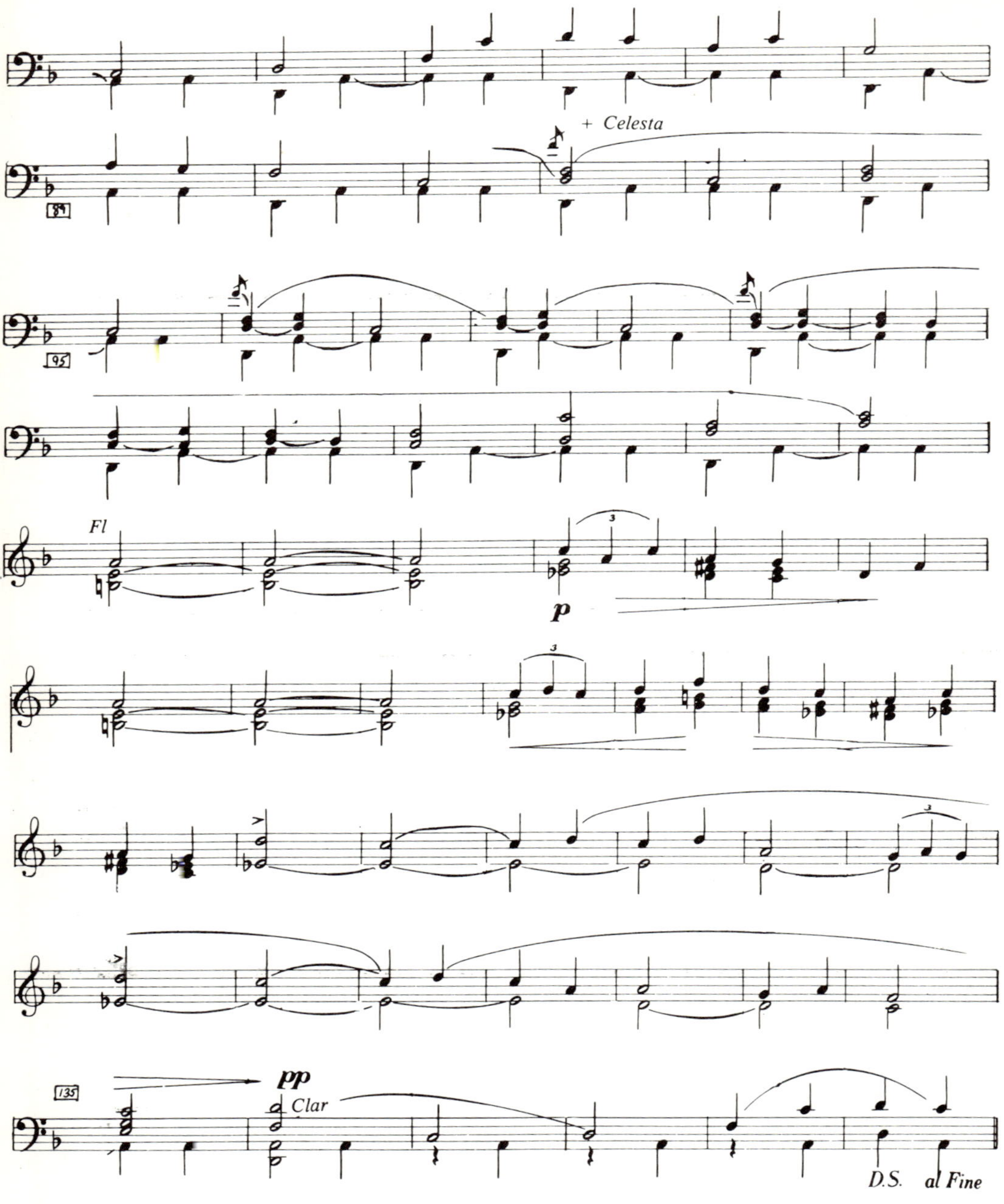

+ Celesta
89
95
Fl
p
135
pp
Clar
D.S. al Fine

Suite in D major for Orchestra

J.S. Bach 1685-1750

Orchestra	Oboe	2	Strings
	Trumpet	3	Continuo (Harpsichord)
	Timpani		

It is not known when this suite was written, but it was performed in Leipzig late in Bach's career. After his death most of Bach's music was forgotten. Mendelssohn, who 're-discovered' Bach gave this suite its next performance in 1832, in Leipzig.

The suite has five contrasting movements, all in D major. This formula is the forerunner of *sonata-form*. The small orchestra is a reminder of the limited means available to a composer then. The keyboard instrument is used to fill out the gaps in the orchestral sound. Music written for such an orchestra does not have the dynamic range or the colour of a modern symphony orchestra.

Overture

Bars

1-24   Stately introduction which has a dotted rhythm.

24-107   Fugue in duple time. A *fugue* is like a musical game in which two or more players *(voices)* chase each other, and combine, according to set rules. (As no voice should be omitted from a fugue, the arrangement given here can only indicate some of the musical ideas.)

24-42   Exposition. The voices enter in descending order.
subject: the first voice to enter *(24)*.
answer: the same idea, entering later *(25, 28, 29)*.
countersubject: accompanies the answer *(25, 28, 29)*.

42-88   Middle section or development.
Episode: a section which is independent of the subject *(42-50)*.
Subject, accompanied by a broad woodwind melody *(50-58)*.
Further development of the subject. There is everchanging tonality, but Bach does not modulate far from the home key *(58-71)*.
Episode, with new comments from the oboe, followed by subject and woodwind melody as before *(71-89)*.

89-107   Recapitulation; based on the exposition with new orchestration.

107-122   An inversion of the introduction in common time.

Air

An all-time favourite often heard arranged as a violin solo *(Air on a G string)*. In the original, the three upper voices engage in conversation over a bass which moves firmly in octaves.

In Bach's day it was usual for players to add their own ideas to the written notes of the composer. Indeed, sometimes the composer only wrote the broad outline of his musical ideas and left the details to the players. Some conductors revive this idea by making the repeats more ornamental.

Gigue
A lively dance movement to conclude the suite.

Concerto in E♭ major for Trumpet

Josef Haydn 1732-1809

	Flute	2	Trumpet	2	Strings
Orchestra	Oboe	2	Horn	2	
	Bassoon	2	Timpani		

Aged sixty-four and shortly after returning from a second visit to London, Haydn wrote his one and only trumpet concerto. While Haydn was away, Anton Weidinger, a Viennese trumpeter, had developed a keyed trumpet which was a big improvement on the 'natural' trumpet. It is reasonable to assume that this break-through aroused Haydn's interest in the trumpet as a solo instrument. The concerto is designed to demonstrate the technical superiority of Weidinger's instrument. It features chromatic work *(bar 66)*, and long rapid passages *(bar 107)*: all quite impossible on the old 'natural' instrument. The keyed trumpet had a short life, however, as the invention of the valve trumpet in 1813, brought the instrument to its present form.

First Movement
Bars
- **1-36** Orchestral opening based on the first subject. During this the soloist sounds a single note and then makes two brief entries. The solo part is demanding even by modern standards. If one imagines the anxiety of the player — probably Weidinger — at the first performance, the first real test of his new instrument, it may explain these unusual entries which allow the player to test his instrument unnoticed by the audience.
- **37-93** The solo trumpet enters properly with a statement of the first subject. The second subject *(60)*, begins like the first, but ends with a descending chromatic figure.
- **93-125** Development, beginning with the subject in C minor. After brilliant solo passages *(107)*, the orchestra rounds off the section.
- **125-173** Recapitulation, based on the first subject. The triplet passage *(143)* produces variety. The soloist may perform a cadenza *(168)*; then follows the orchestral coda.

Quintet for Piano and Strings in A major

Franz Schubert 1797-1828

Ensemble   Violin, Viola, Cello, Bass, Piano.

This work was commissioned by an amateur cellist and written when Schubert was twenty-two. Two years previously he had composed his first version of 'The Trout', and he used that melody again in the fourth movement of this suite. The work is popularly known as the 'Trout' Quintet. Schubert wrote an easy part for the cello but gave it some of the catchiest music.

The variations are inventive in colour and texture, but seldom loose sight of the main theme.

Theme and Variations

Theme   For strings only

Variation   I   Theme with more ornaments, on a high register of the piano. The strings have a triplet figure.

Variation II   Theme on viola with triplet figure on violin. Piano intrudes to emphasise parts of the theme.

Variation III   Cello plays theme. Violin and viola provide a rhythmic background while the piano runs riot.

Variation IV   Change of key to D minor. A forceful treatment of the theme, its rhythm is very prominent. In the second section the five parts imitate each other with much dynamic interest.

Variation V   In B♭ major. The other instruments accompany the cello. The second section explores distant keys before returning to D major.

Allegretto   A presentation of the theme as in the song. The cello has the honour of ending the movement.

The Hebrides (Fingal's Cave) Overture

F. Mendelssohn 1809-1847

Orchestra	Flute	2	Horn	2
	Oboe	2	Trumpet	2
	Clarinet	2	Timpani	
	Bassoon	2	Strings	

Being a rich man's son, Mendelssohn finished his education at the age of twenty with a 'grand tour' of Europe. The first part of his tour took him to Britain. His letters show that he loved the wild beauty of Scotland. In this overture he portrays the scottish seascape in sound, as many other people had done on canvas and in poetry. The music conveys to the imagination the restless nature of the sea, in calm and tempestuous moods, with glimpses of sailing boats and the activities of wild life. However, it is for each listener to interpret exactly what Mendelssohn is describing at any particular time. The melody-lines, the rhythms, the marvellous sound-colours and the dynamic effects all merit careful listening.

Bars

1-92   Exposition. The main idea of the work is stated in the B minor opening bar. With shifting tonality, it swells against a backdrop of sustained chords.

A transition passage *(34)* follows in which there are stormy outbursts leading to the second subject in D major *(47)*. This is a tranquil duo for cello and bassoon under a tremulando figure before being taken up by the violins *(57)*. The first subject reappears *(70)* in a variety of moods. The end of the exposition is marked by four emphatic bars.

93-177 The development section, beginning with the first subject, is announced by a fanfare for brass. The second subject makes a brief appearance *(123)* to be cast aside by the first *(135)*. This is given a variety of treatments before leading to the climax *(169)*. The section ends with the figure which closed the exposition.

178-216 Recapitulation. There is new orchestration of the old ideas. The second subject is heard on the clarinet (marked *very tranquil*) with a sustained accompaniment.

217-268 Large-scale coda. Tempo is stepped up and new ideas are heard. The first subject returns and rises to a turbulent climax. Suddenly, sunshine breaks through and brings the piece to a calm ending.

Mother Goose Suite

Maurice Ravel 1875-1937

Orchestra	Flute	2	Kettledrum
	Piccolo	1	Triangle
	Oboe	2	Cymbals
	Cor Anglaise	1	Bass drum
	Clarinet	2	Gong
	Bassoon	2	Xylophone
	Double bassoon	1	Glockenspiel
	Horn	1	Celesta
			Harp
			Strings

Ravel was an impressionist. Orchestral colour and texture are very important in this idiom, but Ravel uses melody more than other impressionists. This work was written in 1908 to illustrate stories from the *Mother Goose* collection for the children of a friend. The stories are by different writers and are not connected. Generally, the music sets the mood and does not describe the events. The pentatonic mode is used extensively.

Ravel wrote the work as a piano duet (with one easy part) but he later orchestrated it as a ballet suite.

Pavan for the Sleeping Beauty

A *pavan* is a solemn processional dance, sometimes danced in memory of the dead.

The motif of the first bar creates an atmosphere of childlike wonder. A second melody intertwines with it *(9)*. Great sensitivity is felt in the orchestration and the use of discords.

Tom Thumb

As he wandered through the forest, Tom Thumb scattered crumbs to mark his path. But birds picked the crumbs and Tom Thumb was lost.

The changing accent and the uncertain tonality suggest the feeling of being lost. The Tom Thumb theme *(4)* seems to go around in circles because there is no cadence. At bar *50,* the music imitates the action of the birds.

Laideronnette, Empress of the Pagodes

For this piece, Ravel calls on the more exotic instruments of the orchestra: Xylophone, Glockenspiel, Celesta, Kettledrums, Cymbals and Gong.

The story is set in the world of the Pagodes — the 'little people' of french folklore. While their empress bathes, her subjects entertain enthusiastically on tiny instruments made from nutshells.

Although full of fun and games the music is delicate and brittle, as befits the nature of the characters.

Bars

1-7	Introduction.
8-22	Cheerful flute solo over the opening figure.
23-31	Interruptions by the other excitable musicians.
32-54	Oboe tune with distinctive rhythm leads to a quiet interlude which ends with a glissando on the celesta.
55-68	Fun erupts (people often play this tune on the piano with two fingers.)
69-140	A similar tune, but broadened, is taken up by various instruments. It leads to a repeat from *bar 8* with a much fuller orchestration.

Exercise

(i)   Compare and contrast the musical styles of:
  (a)   Bach and Ravel/Schubert/Haydn/Mendelssohn.
  (b)   Haydn and Mendelssohn/Ravel/Schubert.
  (c)   Schubert and Mendelssohn/Ravel.
  (d)   Mendelssohn and Ravel.

(ii) Write biographical notes on Bach/Haydn/Schubert/Mendelssohn/Ravel.

Class Notes/Observations/Analysis

3 —The Growth of Music to 1800

OVERVIEW

There are five periods in European musical history during which distinct styles emerged. Historians rather than musicians gave the names to many of these periods, for nearly every composer thought himself 'modern' in his time. The three middle periods are named after the styles of art, architecture or literature which were popular during those years.

A broad plan of musical history is useful, provided one remembers that it is only a general guide. Composers were not bound by it, as shown, for example, by Bizet's *Symphony in C,* which, although written during the "Romantic" period, (in 1855), is "Classical" in style.

A GENERAL GUIDE

Period	Features of Style
Early music (to 1600)	Discovery and experiment.
Baroque (1600–1750)	Ornamental, with a wealth of detail.
Classical (1750–1800)	Simple and direct, beauty of form.
Romantic (1800–1900)	Expresses human emotions and the beauty of nature.
20th Century Music	Another period of experiment.

EARLY MUSIC TO 1600

Plainchant, the official music of the Roman Catholic Church, goes back to St. Ambrose (4th Century). The music, as used today, was collected by Pope Gregory (540-604). This collection is referred to as **Gregorian Chant.** Its purpose was to transmit the message of the Sacred Scriptures. **The melodies imitated the pronunciation of the Latin words; there was no regular accent or beat; plainchant was sung unaccompanied and in unison.** It can be noted here that Folk-song and dance have a regular rhythm, but the melodies often came from religious music.

Even before the tenth century attempts were made to notate music. A pitch line had symbols *(neums)* written above or below it as the melody rose or fell. **Staff notation** grew from this simple idea. Guido d'Arrezo, an Italian monk is credited with the invention, about 1000 A.D. The 'Great Stave' covered the vocal range from bass to soprano. The Treble and Bass clef system, as now used, is easier to read.

Pitch line
(1000 A D)　　　　　　　*Great stave*　　　　　　*Treble and bass clefs*

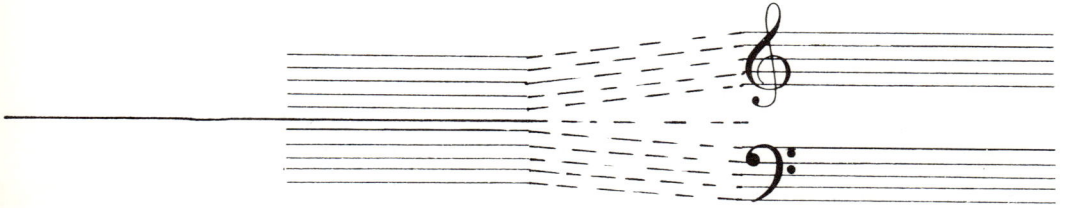

After the 10th Century, singers tried to find a satisfactory way of harmonising a melody. The natural differences of male and female voices led to a crude system called the **Organum.** It was simply another vocal line, parallel to the melody, a fourth or fifth apart. For example:

By the 12th century musicians had learned to combine different melodies successfully **(Counterpoint).** The progress from the Organum to the difficulties of Counterpoint was very great. The first known example dates from about 1300 and is quoted here:

SUMER IS ICUMEN IN (A round for six voices)

(courtesy of the British Library, London)

Summer is a coming in, loudly sing cuckoo,
Groweth seed and bloweth mead and springeth the word anew.
Sing cuckoo.
Ewe bleateth after lamb, cattle loweth too,
Bullock sterteth, buck verteth, merrily sing cuckoo.

The *Renaissance* (1350-1500) fostered music in addition to the other arts. Musical events were promoted and musicians were patronised in the stately homes of the wealthy. It was because instruments had improved so much that people began to enjoy instrumental music without words or dance. Groups of friends, who used to come together for an evening of singing, now preferred to play their songs on instruments, and composers worked to provide interesting pieces for them.

A medieval musical group. The keyboard player is Orlando de Lassus.

Larousse

Music was *the* fashionable pastime of the wealthy and educated classes. The rulers set the example. King Henry VIII was an expert composer and a skilled lute player; Queen Elizabeth played the virginals. Stately homes had resident musicians and every English lady and gentleman was able to sing, dance and accompany songs on the lute.

Contrapunctual music was most popular because with this, each member of the group had an interesting tune to play. Staged entertainments, like **masques** and **pageants,** paved the way for Oratorio and Opera.

The religious strife known as the *Reformation* was to leave its mark on the progress of music. Martin Luther (1483-1546), himself a good composer, tried to bring the people closer to God through music. He loved to hear a congregation sing and he wrote simple hymns in the language of the people. This move was resisted by the Catholic Church at the *Council of Trent* (1545), because it considered plainchant to have been divinely given for worship. **Polyphonic music,** sung in Latin, was allowed however, and composers like Palestrina and de Lassus wrote magnificent choral music for church liturgy. From this time, the **organ** was the only instrument of accompaniment allowed. A golden age of organ building and composing for organ followed in the "Baroque period".

Composers of this period

Orlando de Lassus 1532-1594
Palestrina 1525-1594
Thomas Morley 1557-1603

Victoria 1548-1611
William Byrd 1543-1623

BAROQUE MUSIC 1600-1750

Baroque Organ in the Saint Bavo Church, Haarlem. (courtesy of the Royal Netherlands Embassy)

The music of this period is described as **Baroque,** because it is like baroque art and architecture; **very ornate, splendid and colourful.**

Features of Baroque Music include:

> (i) Melodies were very **ornamental.**
> (ii) Forms were very **complex,** *e.g.* the fugue.
> (iii) The texture was **contrapuntal.**

Stories from the Scriptures were unfolded dramatically in **oratorio.** Bach and Handel were the great writers in this form. It was only a matter of time before oratorio moved to the theatre and **opera** was born. Now, on stage, the singers acted out the drama in costume. The plots of early operas were taken from the ancient classics rather than from the Scriptures. Orchestral and instrumental music multiplied. This, and the popularity of operatic arias and art-songs, encouraged the growth of **homophonic** (single melody) **music.**

Composers from this period

Monteverdi (1567-1643)   Bach (1685-1750)
Lully (1632-1687)   Handel (1685-1759)
Buxtehude (1637-1707)   Scarlatti (1685-1757)
Corelli (1653-1713)   Vivaldi (1678-1741)
Purcell (1659-1695)

Exercise

(i)   List the main features of Baroque Music. Refer to a particular part of Bach's music which illustrates each feature.

(ii) Write a note on the development of music notation.

JOHANN SEBASTIAN BACH 1685-1750

Life

Seven generations of Bachs were prominent musicians. A native of Eisenach in North Germany, Johann Sebastian was brought up a strict Protestant and he remained a man of religion all his life. An orphan at ten, he had little encouragement to learn music. At the age of fifteen, he entered the choir school at Luneburg, where he soon began to shine. He was so keen that he once walked the 200 miles to Lubeck, to attend the famous Musical Evenings organised by Buxtehude!

His first important post was at Weimar, where he worked for nine years from 1708. During this time he produced many of his instrumental and orchestral works. In 1717 he secured the post of Kapellmeister (organist and choirmaster) at St Thomas' Church, Leipzig. For the remaining thirty years of his life, the loft of St Thomas' was his throne. He won fame, not so much as a composer, but as the greatest living organist. It was his duty to write music for the church ceremonies. Week after week he turned out new compositions which were heard once and then cast aside. On his death, his collection of manuscripts barely escaped burning along with his other personal effects. Much of his music was lost because it was used by local traders as wrapping paper.

Bach was also an expert on organ design and construction. One of his pleasures was to act as consultant on the designing and building of many of the fine church organs of this time. But there was little time spent away from his post. His duties were heavy and the pay small, and he worked hard to provide for his large family. His employers expected him to teach Latin on top of his music duties. It was a task which he did grudgingly and he was often reprimanded on this account.

Music

Bach's advances in harmony and in the tuning of keyboard instruments were so important that all musicians since his time are indebted to him. His musical output was staggering in its perfection and in its quantity. He wrote in almost every possible form, except opera. Bach's musical style is **Baroque** in the **complex counterpoint** of his

Bach advises an organ builder

organ and **choral** works, but he moves towards the **Classical** style in his **songs** and **instrumental** works, where **melody** becomes most important **(homophonic).**

Works

Church music *St Matthew Passion; Mass in B Minor; Christmas Oratorio*
Orchestral *Brandenburg Concertos; Suites*
Clavier *The Forty-eight Preludes and Fugues; French Suites; etc.*
Organ *Preludes; Fugues; Toccatas; etc.*
Songs, Cantatas and Instrumental works *Suites for Violin and Cello*

GEORGE FREDRICK HANDEL 1685-1759

Life

The year 1685 gave two great composers to the world — Bach and Handel. Both men came from the same part of Germany, but their lives followed very different courses, and they were never destined to meet. While Bach beavered his life away within the confines of a cathedral square and struggled to make ends meet, bachelor Handel lived more like a 20th century executive than an 18th century musician. He promoted and managed spectacular music projects, sometimes successfully, sometimes not. He made and lost fortunes and numbered royalty among friends and enemies alike.

Handel's father, a barber/doctor in Halle, only tolerated music lessons if they did not interfere with school progress. Handel managed to keep up his school work and also learn organ, harpsichord, violin and oboe. Before he was eleven, his teachers advised that he be sent to Italy to study music. His father rejected this 'nonsense' and decided instead that his son should make the family fortune as a solicitor. Handel submitted for a time but eventually threw up law and began his career as a musician in Hamburg. Competition was keen, and once he even fought a duel to keep a music job!

Since he had first heard of Italy, it had been Handel's dream to go there and study **opera** in its birthplace. At twenty-one he could restrain himself no longer, and so he set off, unknown and penniless, for Italy. His instinct proved sound, however, and within three years his reputation soared and he had offers of jobs from London and Hanover. He took the Hanover job, as Kapellmeister at the Elector's court. He was invited to stage an opera in London, which he did with great success. On a second visit to London in 1713, he was welcomed like a hero. The Queen pressed him to stay, and, when his leave was over, he refused to return, breaking his contract with Hanover. The following year the Queen died. To Handel's dismay, the newly appointed king was the Elector of Hanover, who became George I. For a time he was in disgrace, but he was such an important personality that the king could not do without him. George forgave him and doubled his salary. The King got good value in return, with works like the *Water Music* and the *Fireworks Music* for state occasions.

For the next twenty years Handel put all his effort into Italian opera. With boundless energy he wrote opera after opera, dashing across Europe to scout for singers, returning in time to produce, direct and manage his shows. This activity brought mixed returns. Handel's success caused jealousy and his rivals used many "dirty tricks" to ruin his career. Handel had produced over forty operas before he had to admit failure.

Now in h s fifties and in debt, he suffered a stroke. Where others would have given in, Handel looked for new outlets. He turned to **oratorio** and it proved to be his best mode of expression. He achieved instant success and for another twenty years he turned out an average of one great oratorio a year. Nearing sixty, his robust health again began to flag. Seeking a cure, he set out for Germany, was seriously injured in a carriage accident and lost his eyesight as a result of an operation (by coincidence, his surgeon had also operated unsuccessfully on Bach's eyes). Returning to England, he fought on, composing by dictation, performing and conducting from memory.

He died as he lived, emersed in his work. He collapsed when conducting a charity performance of *Messiah*. His funeral was as spectacular as his own operas. His tomb is in Westminister Abbey, among the great and famous of England.

Music

People never tire of comparing the work of Bach and Handel. Both were Baroque composers, but quite different. Handel's music reflects his basic good humour. It is **moving and eloquent, requiring large forces of singers and players** for best effect. It is more **simple and direct** than Bach's and less complicated. Beethoven said of Handel

'He achieved great effects through simple means'.

Works

Oratoria *Messiah* (The story of Jesus, written in 23 days, firs- performed in Fishamble Street, Dublin, 1742.) *Samson; Judas Maccabeus.*
Opera (40) *Rinaldo; Serse;* Others rarely played.
Orchestral *Water Music; Fireworks Music; Concerti Grosso.*
Organ and Harpsichord *Concertos; Sonatas; etc.*

Neal's Music Hall in Fishamble Street, Dublin, where Handel's 'Messiah' was first performed.

CLASSICAL MUSIC 1750-1800

Simple and **graceful** are words to describe Classical architecture as well as Classical music.

The Panthenon (Athens) — regular in form like Classical Music.

Features of Classical Music include:

(i) The main interest is in **melody.** It is **elegant** and **polite.**

(ii) The melody is accompanied by **blocks of harmony** (the opposite to polyphony).

(iii) The melody is built from **regular four-bar phrases.**

(iv) **Harmony is simple** (confined to Primary and Secondary triads).

(v) **Rhythm** is very **regular** and does not draw attention to itself.

(vi) **Forms** are also **regular** and bound by **exact rules.**

(vii) **Modulation is confined** to closely related keys.

Texture

The heavy **texture** of polyphonic music lost favour in this period to the clear texture of **homophonic** (melody, clearly heard over a background of block harmony and steady rhythm). Haydn was the first great classical composer and he explored the full range of orchestra textures then possible. Orchestral instruments had improved greatly and brass players were by now regular members of the orchestra. The keyboard was no longer needed.

Form

The **sonata, symphony** and **string quartet** became the most used forms in the Classical period.

Composers

A vast amount of music was written in the classical style by a host of excellent classical composers. Many of these would have been better remembered had they not been overshadowed by the brilliance of Haydn and Mozart. Some of these lesser known composers include:

    Clementi 1752-1832
    Hummel 1778-1837
    Czerny 1791-1857

Exercise

Find examples of the main features of Classical style, either in *Haydn's Trumpet Concerto* or in *The Sailor's Song.*

JOSEF HAYDN 1732-1809

Life

Born into a wheelwright's family in an Austrian village, Josef and his brother Michael, showed, from infancy, a great talent for singing. Their father, a simple man and a good singer, was pleased with the village fame of his sons, little realising that both would achieve European fame. When he was eight years old, Josef was awarded a place in the Cathedral school in Vienna. Although his training was mainly in singing, he also composed, whenever he got the chance. When his voice broke, he was dismissed from the school and had to fend for himself. He set up in Vienna as a music teacher and at the same time taught himself violin, clavier and composition. Hard work and self-discipline were his masters, as well as advice from whatever quarter he could get it.

He composed a lot of music for the assorted groups of musicians he knew. His pieces were written in a four-movement form, the first movement of which became the framework of **Sonata Form.** At the age of twenty-seven he secured his first regular job — musical director of a minor landowner's twelve-man orchestra. He put his heart into what he thought would be his life's work. Settling down, he married a woman who was to be the scourge of his life. A year later, his master got into financial difficulties and the musicians were the first to be let go.

Haydn's skill had been noted by neighbouring Prince Esterhazy, who now hired him. For the next thirty years Haydn wore the Esterhazy livery. Lavish entertaining was the prince's passion. He built a remote castle in the mountains, called Esterhaze, which was designed just for entertaining. The court spent about half of every year there and the musical entertainment provided came to be regarded as one of the great treats for guests. The orchestra and choir improved under Haydn and he was able to try out new ideas as soon as he thought of them. The Prince gave him a free hand to seek and hire the best musicians in Europe. Few composers have enjoyed such ideal conditions. The only possible shadow was that, being servants, musicians were separated from their families. This suited Haydn, however. A man of routine and regular habits, he thrived on the monastic life, and his servant status did not injure his pride.

By 1791, Haydn's old master had died and his young successor sacked all the musicians. Haydn was quite wealthy and had been left a good pension, but he was not yet ready to retire. An invitation to provide a season of music in London attracted him. On his arrival there, he found himself a celebrity. His life of sincere and dedicated work was given public recognition, which he accepted graciously and with mild surprise. Twice he visited London and this part of his life witnessed the composition of his greatest symphonies. In retirement, he wrote his greatest oratorios — *The Seasons* and *The Creation.*

Now in his seventies, he delighted in the stream of distinguished visitors who called on him. Since his London visits, Haydn had a special ambition. He longed to write a national Anthem for Austria, which would equal England's *"God Save the King"*. The result was *The Emperor's Hymn:*

This tune became his proudest achievement. When he was dying he asked to be carried to his piano, where he played it over several times.

Music

Haydn was always correct in appearance and manner. He would not dream of sitting down to work without wearing his wig. His handwriting was also neat, and when asked how he managed his huge output, he replied that he would sketch a complete structure in the morning and finish the details in the afternoon. Before he wrote anything, he had it fully worked out in his mind so that his first copy was usually also the last. Always a devout man, each of his compositions begins and ends with a prayer.

His long career lasted from the Baroque period well into the Romantic. His music, however, was **Classical** in the strict sense. When one looks at the course of music in Europe during his lifetime, it is clear that he laid down the ground-rules of the Classical style. He established the *quartet,* and the *symphony* as the best large-scale form and left many examples of how it should be used. The symphony orchestra developed on his four-section plan. His pioneering work earned him the title **"The Father of the Symphony"**. Although his life was one of service, his art was totally independent. He wrote in his diary:

"Art is free and should be fettered by no mechanical regulation . . . . . . the educated ear is the sole authority on all these questions."

Works

Symphonies (104)
Some are named after interesting features, *e.g. The Farewell, The Clock, The Drum Roll, The Surprise, The Toy, etc.*
   Chamber Music 83 string quartets; Trios; *etc.*
   Concertos c. 50 for piano and other solo instruments.
   Church Music Masses; *Stabat Mater; etc.*
   Oratorio *The Seasons; The Creation; etc.*
Also: Opera (20); **Songs; Keyboard and Instrumental music.**

ESTERHAZY CASTLE

(courtesy of the Austrian Embassy)

WOLFGANG AMADEUS MOZART
1756-1791

Life

Probably one of the most gifted of all the great names in history. His father was a prominent composer, who served the Archbishop of Salzburg. Only two of the seven Mozart children survived and, when they realised that both had amazing musical ability, the parents made it their life's work to nurture it. Their progress was rapid and they were soon ready for a concert tour of Europe. Besides giving recitals, they were exhibited like circus freaks. In London they were billed:

> Miss Mozart of 11 and Master Mozart of 7
> Prodigies of Nature

The public was invited to view them between the hours of two and five, to test their father's claims. For a fee of half-a-crown, one could set them tasks in sight-reading, improvisation and playing blindfolded.

When he was fourteen Mozart was taken on a tour of Italy. His boyhood compositions were already causing a stir and his amazing memory was evident when he wrote down the full score of an oratorio from memory, after one hearing! Later Mozart took over his father's position in Salzburg, but his independent nature sparked off rows and he was dismissed, being kicked onto the street on the Archbishop's orders. He never again held a secure job.

As his father had always feared, Mozart's flame burned out quickly and he died at the age of thirty-five. The cause of death is not certain; various sources suggest overwork and worry, typhus, or poisoning by a jealous rival. Some weeks before he died, a mysterious visitor in a black cloak commissioned a *Requiem,* leaving a purse of gold in payment. Listening to the music one can easily believe that it comes from the heart of a man who knew he would soon meet his maker. His last request to his wife was that his death be kept secret for a few days, until a friend's financial difficulties were resolved. His burial was unattended by mourners and he was laid in a common grave for paupers.

The birthplace of Mozart, in Salzburg
(courtesy of the Austrian Embassy)

Music

Although many worries and little security came his way, Mozart always kept his best side for his public and was high-spirited in company. He liked to claim that he was a better dancer than a musician. His output of work is extraordinary, yet he rarely gave the impression of being busy. Great music seemed to come to him easily and distractions did not affect him. He could jot down ideas during a game of billiards, or he could write happily in the noisy market-place. Once, in a boarding house with other musicians, he said that the mixture of sounds as they practised gave him a wealth of ideas. A great work like *The Marriage of Figaro* took only fourteen days to write, and the overture was only started on the night before the opening performance. Yet works like that and the *Jupiter Symphony* are so perfect that they could not be improved upon. He did admit that, like Haydn, an entire work was fully organised in his mind before any writing was done.

Recent discoveries show that Mozart received enormous fees for his work, but he was a compulsive gambler and money flowed through his hands. Michael Kelly, the Irish tenor, who was a friend and pupil, said that music lessons were often spent at the billiard table. It was on billiards and skittles that Mozart gambled away most of his earnings. His wife and child, whom he adored, lived an unsettled life, under constant threat of want. Mozart's letters are a litany of requests for 'one last loan' to clear his debts.

Mozart's music is the perfect example of **Classical** style. His gift for melody was greater than Haydn's and he used the *Symphony* and *quartet* form with much more expressiveness and depth. His orchestration was so well balanced that each section of the orchestra can be clearly heard. His operas look forward to the work of Wagner in their treatment of character and atmosphere.

Works

Symphonies (50) *Haffner; Prague; Linz; Jupiter.*
Concertos (26) *For Piano; Horn; Flute; Violin.*
Operas (20) *The Magic Flute; Don Giovanni; The Marriage of Figaro.*
Sonatas For Violin; Piano; and other solo instruments.

Also: Songs; Quartets.

4 —Romantic Music 1800-1900

Principles of Romantic Art and Literature

Love of Nature, which is seen as vast and powerful
Mood and Atmosphere captured
Freedom of imagination
Free range given to emotions, even passion
Colour and Drama
Free form, with 'ordinary language' used in poetry
The poet or artist often sees the life of the simple peasant as the ideal one.

'. . . (poetry is) . . the spontaneous overflow of powerful feelings. . .'
W. Wordsworth (Romantic Poet).

'. . . thou art pouring forth thy soul abroad
In such an ecstasy . .'
John Keats (Romantic Poet).

The Cornfield   *(courtesy of The National Gallery, London)*   **John Constable**

'. . . by a close observation of Nature, (the artist) discovers qualities existing in her which have never been portrayed before'. Constable (Romantic Artist).

Features of Romantic Music include:

---

1. Melody is **freed from rules** to express human emotions.
2. Harmony is adventurous, with **discords** and **modulation** to remote keys.
3. **Rhythm** itself becomes **a means of expression.** Music slows, speeds up or stops as the mood demands — unlike the strict 'sewing-machine' rhythm of classical music.
4. Classical forms are still used but they are **changed** as the composer wishes.

Music of this period is called 'Romantic' because it had many things in common with the poetry of Romantic poets like Shelley, Wordsworth and Keats. These poets were intensely interested in the meaning of life and nature. Human emotions were also of great importance to them. While classical composers needed no other title for their works than a number *(Opus 2, No. 1, Sonata in D, etc.),* Romantic composers often gave descriptive names to their works showing that they had a message for people, *e.g. 1812 Overture; Spring Sonata; Moonlight Sonata; etc.* Even if some of these names were only given later by listeners, they show that some story or lesson was expected from the music. A multitude of different musical forms appears, all shaped according to the emotional needs of each composer, rather than following strict rules.

Beethoven's career is a bridge between the classical and the romantic periods. His early work is classical but, as it goes on, his music becomes more personal. *The Pastoral Symphony* clearly expresses human emotions and the changing face of nature. **Concertos** explored the technical possibilities of the improved instruments and the increasing skill of the players. The symphonies of composers like Beethoven and Brahms were epic works while the **symphonic poems** of Liszt, Berlioz and Strauss, moved from the classical layout to the closely woven single-movement work, with a main theme which runs right through **(leitmotif).** Art-song, **opera** and **ballet** flourished because they were ideal forms for self-expression.

Orchestral instruments reached their present state of development early in the 19th Century and the grouping of players into four sections became the rule. The great professional orchestras were being established at this time and the acceptance of the conductor's authority raised the standard of orchestral performance to a very high level. The scoring now made demands on players in every section that could no longer be met by amateur players.

Romantic Composers

Instrumental Music

Beethoven 1770-1827
Paganini 1782-1840
Schubert 1797-1828
Berlioz 1803-1869
Mendelssohn 1809-1847
Chopin 1810-1849
Schumann 1810-1856
Liszt 1811-1886
Lalo 1823-1892
Brahms 1833-1897
Saint Saens 1835-1921

Art Song

Schubert 1797-1828
Schumann 1810-1856

Brahms 1833-1897
Faure 1845-1924
Wolf 1860-1903
Mahler 1860-1911

Opera

Weber 1786-1826
Rossini 1792-1868
Donizetti 1797-1848
Verdi 1813-1901
Gounod 1818-1893
Offenbach 1819-1880
Bruckner 1824-1896
Bizet 1838-1875
Mussorgsky 1839-1881

NATIONALIST COMPOSERS

The 19th century saw great interest in patriotism and democracy. These ideas are reflected in the literature and music of the time. (A difference can be seen between the political idea of nationalism and the musical. In politics, nationalism often meant 'my country against all others', while in music, pride in one's own culture aroused a desire to **share** it with others.) Romantic composers turned to **folk music** for their inspiration. More than others, the following composers used melody and harmony that were deliberately associated with their native countries:

Russia	Borodin, 1833-1887	
	Mussorgsky,1839-1881	
	Tchaikovsky, 1840-1893	
	Rimsky-Korsakof, 1844-1887	
Norway	Grieg, 1843-1907	
Finland	Sibelius, 1865-1957	
Spain	Albeniz, 1860-1909	
Bohemia	Smetana, 1824-1884	
	Dvorak, 1841-1904	

Russian stamps, honouring not only their own great nationalist composer, Rimsky Korsokov, but also that of nearby Norway, Edvard Grieg.

LUDWIG VAN BEETHOVEN
1770-1827

Life

Life was not kind to Beethoven. A degenerate father made him practise for long hours against his will, paraded him about like another infant Mozart, and lied about his age. As a child he studied at the *Bonn Electoral Court,* where his father was a singer. When he was eleven, he found an inspiring teacher, named Neefe, who was able to train his exceptional talent. Both Haydn and Mozart heard him play and encouraged him. When he was seventeen, his mother died, and he had to support his two brothers and his father, who had by now lost his job.

On his father's death in 1792, Beethoven moved to Vienna to study under Haydn. He quickly outgrew Haydn and other eminent musicians. He was an instinctive composer who needed no other master than his own natural genius.

Before he was thirty, he became aware of growing deafness. In desperation he thought of suicide for a time and he avoided company in an attempt to hide this 'disgrace'. His brusque behaviour was partly a front to avoid admitting that he could not hear what was being said to him. His deafness soon became total and for the rest of his life he communicated with the help of conversation books and worthless hearing trumpets. In appearance he was not favoured either. He was of small stature, and smallpox had left an ugly mark on his face. Some who knew him described him as 'repulsive' and his offer of marriage was rejected by a woman who said that he was 'ugly' and 'half-crazy'.

A portrait of Beethoven on a Rumanian stamp which helps to explain, perhaps, the young lady's unflattering remarks.

Living accomodation was a constant problem for him. He made forty-four moves during his years in Vienna! He reduced each of his lodgings, with incredible speed, to a state of squalor. Thanks to his father's greed, he was uneducated in every subject but music. As a result, he was slow at arithmetic and writing. For this reason, facts are scarce about his thoughts and theories. His letters show more concern about such things as missing socks than about music. He lied and cheated about money, especially when dealing with music publishers. He could be good humoured and even boisterous on occasion, but he was likely to turn morose and offensive without warning. Despite his boorish manners, his genius won him the respect of all. His admirers stood by him, putting up with his uncontrollable temper and abusive language.

Music

As he progressed into total deafness, Beethoven challenged fate and went on to achieve the impossible. He began to write in the new personal style that was to be called 'Romantic'. Alone in his silent world, he carried out a one-man revolution and created a new world of sound which was crowned by happiness, the joy of life and the beauty of nature. There is little of the depression that he must have suffered. Perhaps he set out to create a fantasy world of music, the opposite of the world that his body inhabited.

Sonata form was the structure that he used to best effect. In his hands, it becomes very expressive, the development sections being very long and inventive. In harmony his work does not progress far beyond Mozart but he uses the same principles to greater effect. In melody and modulation he advanced greatly. His orchestra is much larger than before with a greater range of dynamics and tone colour. The most important advance is Beethoven's treatment of **rhythm.** His rhythms can be as important as the melody *(e.g. his 7th Symphony, 4th movement.).* Beethoven wrote masterful works in every form that he used. His string quartets probably reflect the highest points of his self-expression.

Chief works

Symphonies (9) *5th Symphony* (written in 1808, probably reflects the anguish caused by his deafness)
6th Symphony (The Pastoral Symphony), also written in 1808 — a happy work
7th and 9th Symphonies, very great and direct works
Concertos Five for piano (incl. *5th, The Emperor),* also Violin concerto
Overtures *Egmont* and eight others
Piano (32) Sonatas (incl. *Pathetique; Appassionata; Farewell; Moonlight)*
Violin and Cello Sonatas and other works
Opera *Fidelio*
Mass *Missa Solemnis*

NICCOLO PAGANINI 1782-1840

Paganini was a poor boy from Genoa who showed great natural talent for the violin. With the ambition of becoming a great violinist, for five years, from 1801, he devoted himself entirely to technical exercises, never appearing in public during this time. He emerged from his rigorous training to become an idol and a legend in his lifetime. He achieved such unbelievable skill that people firmly believed he had sold his soul to the devil in exchange for it. His nickname *El Diabolo* was apt. A gaunt face was framed by black hair; he was so tall that he dwarfed his instrument, and when he played he became like a man possessed. On his death he was refused a church funeral and five years passed before his body was laid in consecrated ground.

It is now realised that his skill was the result of hard work and a scientific study of his instrument and the muscles used to play it. He advanced the possibilities of violin playing by

   (i) Using a longer fingerboard.
  (ii) Using better strings and bow.
 (iii) Holding the instrument by chin and shoulder, thus leaving the left hand completely free on the fingerboard.
 (iv) Using special bowing techniques, double-stopping, harmonics and other special effects.

Paganini produced a whole library of violin music to display the new techniques he had discovered. His music is very exciting and easy to listen to.

Works

Caprices Studies for violin.
Concert pieces For violin and orchestra.
Violin Concertos

FRANZ SCHUBERT 1797-1828

Schubert was born in Vienna. His father, who was a schoolmaster, first taught him music. All the family was musical and the Schuberts formed their own orchestra. Schubert attended the same choir school as Haydn had and when his voice broke he took up his father's job. But Schubert spent his time scribbling melodies instead of teaching and he soon left the job. He never again held any steady position but lived on the charity of his friends, who were themselves also hard-up artists. He lived and died in poverty and, to all appearances, a failure. During his career he held one successful concert and published one set of songs (he did submit many songs for publication but the publishers rejected them as thrash).

But Schubert's gift for melody was unique. In his short life he wrote over 600 songs, most of which are considered superb by listeners, and a great challenge by singers. Had he lived longer, he would probably have shone in other musical forms also. His potential genius is seen in his short piano pieces and in his *Unfinished Symphony.* Schubert's special music form was the **art-song (lieder)** in which he married **good poetry** to **good melody,** with suitable **accompaniment.** Most of his songs are for solo voice and piano, voice and instrument being of equal importance. The beauty of Nature and all the human emotions are portrayed; there are also dramatic ballads, *e.g. The Erl King,* which tells in song the old story of the 'Other World' people who steal a beautiful child from its parents.

Schubert spent much of his time in the smoke-filled cafes where artists gathered. He often sat close to Beethoven's table, but he was too shy to introduce himself to the man he so admired. He thought it a great honour to be allowed carry a torch at Beethoven's funeral in 1827. Within a year, he himself was to be buried, close to Beethoven, having died from sickness brought on by neglect and careless living habits.

Works

Songs (600) Including the well known *Ave Maria; Whither; Serenade; The Trout*
Song cycles (A group of songs having a common theme and meant to be sung as a unit) — *Die Winterreise; Die Schone Mullerein*
Piano *Impromtus; Moments musicaux*
Instrumental Quartets; Quintets *(The Trout);* Symphonies

A Schubert Evening (Larousse)

ROBERT SCHUMANN
1810-1856

Helping in his father's bookshop in Saxony gave Schumann his love of literature. As a boy, he showed promise as a writer. When his father died in 1825, however, his mother chose law as his profession. At university he became more interested in music than law and eventually devoted himself fully to music. He took lessons from Wieck, an outstanding piano teacher, hoping to become a concert pianist. To make up for lost time, he invented a machine for exercising his fingers. But his invention caused a permanent hand injury and his hopes were ruined.

With some friends he launched a new musical journal, *Die Neue Zeitschrift fur Musik* (The New Journal for Music) in 1834. As editor, his aim was to educate the listening public and to promote new trends in music. The magazine became very influential. His marriage to Clara Wieck, the daughter of his former teacher, was a happy one. She was a brilliant pianist and she made it her mission to present Schumann's music to the public. In his late thirties, Schumann began to suffer mental illness. His powers quickly declined and he was confined to a home where he died at the age of forty-six.

Schumann's music is very personal and romantic. He was a good song-writer, although less gifted than Schubert. His first love remained the piano and his works show that he died before reaching his peak.

Works

Piano	*Carnaval Suite.*
	Album for the Young and other children's pieces
Others	*Quintet for Piano and Strings*
	Songs and song cycles

FELIX MENDELSSOHN
1809-1847

It has been said that Mendelssohn never had a childhood. His millionaire parents planned to leave no gaps in his education. Except for Sundays, his day began at 5 a.m. Private tutors worked in relays to cram him with knowledge; even on family holidays the tutors were part of the retinue. When he began to show musical promise, his parents were overjoyed. The best musicians were brought to him. They were all impressed by his piano-playing and by his compositions (while he, in his diary, dismissed *their* work as 'deplorable'). When he was fifteen his parents moved to a house where he could mount operas and symphony concerts — this house later became the seat of the German Parliament. Surprisingly, Mendelssohn was not spoiled by his upbringing.

A Midsummer Night's Dream Overture was written when he was seventeen. It is the work of a fully mature composer. Three years later, he produced Bach's *St. Matthew Passion* and so began the new interest in Bach's music. He then completed his education with a Grand Tour of historic Europe. Both Italy and Scotland inspired him to write lasting works.

Returning to Germany, he devoted himself to establishing a *Conservatoire of Music* in Leipzig. Although very rich, and happily married with five children, Mendelssohn worked at a feverish pace and it is generally thought that he worked himself into an early grave.

During the sixteen years of his adult career, Mendelssohn travelled a great deal as a conductor and established the conductor's important role of interpeter of music. He also demanded a high standard of playing from orchestras. His own music is light and airy and has a special magical quality. It is **programme** music in the new romantic style. Many of his piano works have become somewhat dated, but his violin concerto is still marvellous to hear. He produced a vast quantity of good music, most of which, however, is seldom heard.

Works

Oratoria *St Paul; Elijah.*
Songs About eighty, (incl. *On wings of Song*)
Orchestra *Italian Overture; Hebrides Overture; Midsummer Nights Dream Overture*
Concerto *Violin Concerto;* also two concertos for piano
Keyboard Piano and organ works, including *Songs without Words*

FREDRICK CHOPIN 1810-1849

As Chopin was growing up in Warsaw, his parents realised that he had great musical promise. His father, who was a teacher, taught him at home, and made sacrifices to get him the best musical training. By the time he was thirteen, he was a brilliant pianist. He then went to secondary school for three years before becoming a full-time music student in Warsaw. The music he began to write was very different from what was being taught in the composition class and before he was twenty he was gaining a reputation as a pianist and composer of great originality.

In 1830 he settled in Paris and never again returned to Poland. Robert Schumann introduced him in the first issue of *Die Neue Zeitschrift* with "Hats off, Gentlemen, a genius". Chopin achieved quick success and wealth. He had been brought up to feel at home in upper class circles and he was accepted as an equal by the aristocracy of Paris. He was 'in fashion' and people paid high fees for the honour of having him as teacher or recitalist in their homes.

However, his health soon began to weaken. He began to suffer constantly form coughing (once his condition was so bad that his death was reported.) An unusual lady, who wrote popular novels under the pen-name George Sand, took him in charge. Quite the opposite to Chopin, she enjoyed shocking people by her unladylike behaviour and her habit of smoking cigars in public. But to Chopin she was a devoted friend, nursing him through illnesses and ensuring that he enjoyed comfortable working conditions during his ten productive years. In 1846, the friendship broke down through a misunderstanding and Chopin never spoke to her again.

In 1848, Chopin foolishly agreed to do a concert tour of England. He had not performed in public for five years and he was so weak that he often had to be carried about. Most of the tour was spent miserably in bed. Broken in health, he returned to Paris, where he died a year later.

Composer and Pianist

Chopin constructed forms to suit his own needs. The *Nocturnes* were **mood pieces,** very **poetic** and often **dreamy.** He took this form from the Irish pianist John Field. His *Studies* help pianists cope with the special difficulties in his music. They are also very brilliant pieces and easy to listen to *e.g. The Revolutionary Study* expresses his anger on hearing that Warsaw had been sacked by Russian forces. The *Waltzes* are fast and exciting; the *Mazurkas* and *Polonaises* are based on Polish rhythms. His few sonatas broke the classical rules to such an extent that even Schumann lost faith in him.

Chopin's music is **emotional** rather than intellectual. He made the piano more **expressive** than any composer before or since. This was partly due to his *rubato* (flexible) treatment of rhythm. His genius was for *melody perfectly arranged for piano.* As a pianist, Chopin was considered Liszt's equal. Although a frail person, neither his music nor his playing betrayed weakness. To hear him play was an unforgettable experience. Besides being powerful and commanding, he could move the listeners to tears. History has therefore named him the **'Poet of the Piano'.**

Works:

Polonaises (16)	Nocturnes (26)
Mazurkas (50)	Studies (27)
Preludes (24)	Impromptus (4)
Waltzes (14)	Ballades (4)

Favourite works include:

Barcarolle; Berceuse; Tarantella; Polonaise in A; Nocturne in E flat; Grande Waltz.

HECTOR BERLIOZ 1803-1869

A French romantic composer, writer and critic, Berlioz's love for an Irish actress inspired his best known work the *Symphonie Fantastique.* It portrays human emotions on a grand scale. His music is stormy and passionate. He added much to the art of orchestration. His *Damnation of Faust* is also a powerful piece of writing.

FRANZ LISZT 1811-1886

Although an important composer, Liszt is better remembered as perhaps the greatest pianist of all time. From an early age, his prowess at the piano attracted notice. Financed by people from his Hungarian village, he had studied in Vienna and Paris before he was thirteen. Although a fully fledged professional, he spent the next two years in retirement, working slavishly on scales and exercises. He emerged from this rigorous training with an unsurpassable mastery of the keyboard.

For an eleven year period, from 1848, he worked in Weimar, making that town a great centre of musical life. His successes included the launching of Wagner's operas. From 1870, he taught in Budapest, putting a whole generation of great pianists through his hands. He is an important link in the interpetation of the early Romantics. He had known them and had heard them perform. The young musicians, whom he trained, worked on into the 20th century, knowing exactly how Beethoven, Chopin and others wished their music to be played.

Unlike Chopin, Liszt loved performing. His playing was breathtaking and he had a preference for difficult and spectacular works. Under his big hands, the newly invented iron-framed pianos assumed the power of a full orchestra. His success brought him great wealth, which he dispensed freely on charities and needy musicians. He was known and loved in the cities and villages of Europe, Russia and Turkey. Nowhere was his sporting nature better proved than in Clonmel. He arrived to find that the organisers had mistakenly billed him for the previous night. There was no hall, no piano and no audience. In the hotel, where he was to stay, Liszt found an upright piano. He sent word out on the streets for anyone who was interested to come. Not only did he give his program but he went on far into the night, playing from memory the requests of his delighted listeners. Next morning, he left, refusing to take any payment.

Liszt's domestic life was a complicated series of love affairs, except for a three year interlude when he embraced the monastic life. Although he was not ordained, he liked to use his clerical title, *Abbé* Liszt, afterwards. He spent the last few years of his life in

Bayreuth, propping up the schemes of Wagner, now his son-in-law. His death was quite out of character, resulting from a chill which was neglected in the excitement of the Bayreuth Festival.

Music

Liszt composed over a thousand works in the Romantic style. For orchestra he developed a new form, the **Symphonic Poem.** His piano works are **exciting** and **brilliant** and are also **very difficult to play.** His fame as a pianist has overshadowed his greatness as a composer.

Works

Piano: Studies (12) Hungarian Rhapsodies (20) Concertos (2) Transcriptions for piano of other composers works *e.g.* Symphonies by Beethoven and Caprices by Paganini
Orchestra Symphonic Poems (14)
Vocal: Songs; Oratoria; Masses

An East German stamp commemorating the Hungarian composer Liszt and his French contemporary Berlioz.

RICHARD WAGNER 1813-1883

Wagner spent more time 'on the run' than any other composer. From start to finish, his life was a series of escapades — political, musical and domestic. His family affairs were so complicated that law suits were still being waged thirty years after his death. Brought up in Leipzig, Wagner was a late starter at music. At school, he saw himself as another Shakespeare, and when he transferred his interest to music, he believed that he could do better than Beethoven. Having studied music for six months, he presented the world with a symphony and two operas. Each was a disaster. But, quite convinced of his genius, Wagner spent the next twenty years writing operas in his own special style. During this time he lived in poverty, spent time in prison, was involved in revolution and fled to Switzerland for safety. He also found time to write a library of works on philosophy and politics. In 1850, Liszt produced Wagner's *Lohengrin* in Weimar. The opera was a resounding success.

But life did not improve for Wagner. The more fiascos he produced, the more he boasted that he was 'destined to bring about an artistic revolution of unrivalled magnitude'. He went on writing a four-opera cycle so ambitious that he would have to build a special theatre before he could stage it. It was not until he was fifty that his luck changed. King Ludwig of Bavaria, a young and somewhat 'unbalanced' monarch, fancied himself as the founder of a new civilization, to be centred in Bavaria. He begged Wagner to come and work for him:

"The mean cares of everyday life I will banish from you forever," he promised. Against all odds, Wagner's dream came true. With Ludwig's help, he built his dream opera house in Bayreuth, and in August 1876, the first complete performance of *The Ring of the Nibelungs* showed the world press, (which Wagner had carefully invited), that a new genius had burst into musical history.

Wagner's success made him even more conceited. He accepted no criticism. He needed special conditions in which to work. His composing room was draped in silk, Wagner entered in flowing gown and sprinkled perfume around before lounging on a couch to wait for inspiration. After an unhappy marriage lasting thirty-four years, he married Cosmina, the daughter of Liszt, whom he had long loved. Only then did he find domestic happiness. Wagner's days of happiness were short-lived however. His ability to squander money had already made Ludwig bankrupt and almost caused a revolution in Bohemia. At the end of his days, he found himself carrying the financial burden of Bayreuth. His worries led to the series of heart attacks from which he died.

The Bayreuth Opera House

The Musician

Against overwhelming odds, Wagner evolved a new art form which he called **Music-Drama.** He saw that the arias of older opera were artificial devices, which held up the dramatic action. In *his* operas, **the music obeys the needs of the plot** and the **vocal line** is often derived from **normal speech.** A cult of Wagnerism emerged, which was duly upheld by his wife, who lived on to 1930. His themes and writings glorify German mythology. Nazi Germany claimed him as a prophet of their ambitions. Hitler was a family friend and promoted Wagner's operas. As a result of this attention, Wagner's works were for a time under a cloud. But under the direction of Wagner's grandchildren, the Bayreuth Festival has regained a new lease of life. Every August, admirers, from all over the world, gather to enjoy the works of Wagner, in the setting designed for that purpose alone.

Works

Opera *Lohengrin*
Die Meistersinger
Parsifal
The Ring of the Nibelungs (The Rhinegold; the Valkyrie; Siegfried; The Dusk of the Gods)
Tannhanser
Tristan and Isolde

JOHANN STRAUSS 1825-1899

Known as the 'Waltz King' of Vienna, Strauss was a gifted violinist with a remarkable flair for **catchy melody** and **good orchestration.** His orchestra provided music for dancing and for dining. As a conductor Strauss had a gift for inspiring the orchestra and the dancers. He wrote countless **waltzes** and **polkas** that are still as fresh as when they were first heard.

When Strauss visited America with his orchestra he was given a hero's welcome. In his honour an orchestra and choir, two thousand strong, waited to perform *The Blue Danube* under his baton. Besides waltzes, Strauss also wrote **operetta** very successfully. Although he confined himself to a popular form and style of music, the great composers of this time regarded Strauss as one of themselves. Brahms, hardly a waltz fan, envied Strauss's gift for melody and considered himself a less gifted composer.

Works

Waltzes *Tales from the Vienna Woods; Wine, Women and Song; Artist's Life*
Operetta *Die Fledermaus; The Gipsy Baron*

A contemporary print of a **galop** *gives an idea of the extent to which dancing was a part of socialising in the 19th century. Notice that the orchestra is led by a violinist.*

JOHANN BRAHMS 1833-1897

A product of the slums of Hamburg, it was Brahms' ambition to be accepted and make good in his native city. During his 'teens he added to the family income and paid for his music lessons by working as a public-house pianist. In his twenties, he was spotted by the famous violinist, Joachim. Schumann gave him valuable publicity and Brahms became a life long friend of the Schumann family. Both Liszt and Wagner helped him to establish himself.

But Hamburg continued to turn its back on the young Brahms. Torn between devotion to his parents and the frustration of being unable to make a living, he moved to Vienna in 1863. There he won quick fame as a pianist, and the completion of his *Requiem,* in 1867, brought him into the ranks of the great composers. Long after the rest of Europe had acknowledged his greatness, Hamburg paid tribute, in 1899, by conferring on him the freedom of the city.

Sharp of tongue and uncertain of temper, Brahms was gruff in appearance and manner. But he was warm-hearted and, remembering how much help he had recieved from fellow musicians, he was generous with encouragement towards other composers. Even when wealthy and successful, Brahms led a simple life. He was at his desk at five every morning and worked through the day, living chiefly on many strong cigars and coffee.

Music

In an age of change, Brahms stuck to old principles. The experiments of Liszt and Wagner did not appeal to him. He was seen by them as another Beethoven and he deliberately **imitated the orchestral sounds of Beethoven.** He used **classical forms** for his biggest works which are **solemn** and **profound.** He also excelled in **light piano works.**

Works

Overtures *Tragic Overture; Academic Festival Overture; Variations on a Theme by Haydn*
Symphonies (4).
Piano Rhapsodies; Dances; Duets; Waltzes
Vocal Hundreds of songs, *e.g. Sontag (Sunday);* and the *Requiem*

GEORGES BIZET 1838-1875

The suite *L'Arlesienne* and the opera *The Pearlfishers* are well known, but it is for his **tragic opera** *Carmen* (1875) alone that Bizet is immortalized. This was the first opera to grapple successfully with **genuine human emotions.** It did not have the kind of characters that the Paris opera-goers liked and the opera was slow to be accepted. Sadly, Bizet died during the first run of *Carmen*.

Carmen

by Georges Bizet

First performed: Paris 1875

The story is set in Seville outside a cigarette factory *(Cigarette Girls' Chorus)*. Carmen, a gipsy girl, falls in love with Don José, who is a guardsman. She sings and dances to attract his attention *(Habenera)*. Being engaged already, he ignores her. In a dispute, Carmen fights with another girl and is arrested. Again, she uses all her charms to attract Don José *(Sequidilla)*. This time she is successful and he helps her to escape.

She hides in a tavern where a famous bullfighter, Escamillo, is boasting of his exploits *(Toreador's Song)*. Don José joins the company and admits that he is hopelessly in love with Carmen *(Flower Song)*. He deserts the army and follows her to a smugglers' den *(Interlude music)*. There, a fortuneteller forecasts disaster for Carmen *(Card Song)*.

The final scene takes place outside the bullfighting arena *(Fight Music)*. Don José finds that Carmen has betrayed him in favour of Escamillo and when she scorns his promise of love, he kills her. The curtain falls with the tragic knowledge that Don José has thrown away his career and his life for nothing.

Programme notes from Bizet's 'Carmen'.

PETER TCHAIKOVSKY 1840-1893

Tchaikovsky was a Russian composer who took up music late in life. Fortunately, a wealthy widow, whom he never met, gave him an allowance, so that he could work full-time as a composer. He became very well known at home and abroad, even visiting the U.S. in 1891.

His great gift was for **melody,** which was often **sentimental,** harmonised with a **rich orchestral sound.** Not a very original composer, his music has nonetheless a wider appeal than that of many greater composers. It is known and enjoyed even by people who do not consider themselves 'musical'. His wonderful music for **ballet** gave that art a great boost.

Works

Ballet Music *Swan Lake; Nutcracker Suite; Sleeping Beauty*
Orchestral *Symphonies (No. 5, Pathethique); Piano Concerto*
Opera *Eugene Onegin*

ANTONIN DVORAK 1841-1904

Dvorak was a Czech composer who attained international standing in his own lifetime. He spent some years as a visiting teacher in America. His symphony *From the New World* was inspired by this visit. It uses Negro and Czech **folk music** *e.g.* the lovely setting of *Goin' Home* in the second movement. Dvorak's music possesses **lyrical melody within traditional forms.**

Works
Symphonies, Violin and Cello **Concertos. Piano and instrumental music** of a lighter nature, and **Songs**

EDVARD GRIEG 1843-1907

Norway's greatest musician was born in Bergen, where his mother taught him piano. He studied in Leipzig from the age of fifteen. When he returned in 1862, he set up as teacher, composer and concert pianist. He found it hard to make a living in Bergen and so he moved to Copenhagen. Here he met Nina Hagerup, who became his wife and inspiration. Returning to Norway in 1867, Grieg resolved to make good as a Norwegian musician. He had known Hans Christian Anderson in Copenhagen, and he hoped to do for Norwegian folk culture what Anderson had done for German folklore.

In 1874 Ibsen, the dramatist, invited Grieg to write music for one of his plays. The *Peer Gynt Suite* was the result, and it marks a turning point in Grieg's career. It was his first real success and it is now better known than the play itself. The Norwegian government appreciated what he was doing and granted him a pension for life, so that he could concentrate on his work as a 'national' composer. Grieg had a fierce love for his country and he did succeed in putting Norway on the cultural map of Europe. He became very well respected abroad and toured widely conducting his own works. When he died, his tomb was set high in a cliff overlooking a fiord and within sight of his home.

Grieg was a **romantic** in the old tradition. He did not cause any new trends in music but he wrote with great **beauty** and **feeling.** He is sometimes called the 'Chopin of the North'. The opening movement of the *Peer Gynt Suite (Morning)* describes to perfection the rising sun and the awakening of day. His *Piano Concerto* is one of the world's best loved works. It was written when Grieg was twenty-seven. He showed the score to Liszt who said, "Carry on, my friend, you have real talent." Grieg also wrote a number of fine **songs.**

Works

Suites	*Peer Gynt Suite*
	Holberg Suite
Concertos	*Piano Concerto in A minor*
	Lyric Pieces for Piano
	Songs (143)

5-Impressionism and After

IMPRESSIONISM

Claude Monet   *(courtesy of The National Gallery of Ireland)*   **Autumn Scene**

Impressionism is one of the many experiments which took place in the music of this century, and it has had lasting success. Early in the century, Paris was the cradle of Impressionism when artists like Monet and Manet tried to paint objects as they appeared to the eye, rather than as they were in reality, *(e.g.* if one looks at a distant tree, one does not see every branch and leaf clearly, one sees a blur of colour and shade). It was this effect that the Impressionists tried to record onto canvas. They were very keen to catch the effect of light on the object: the same tree may appear different, depending on the kind of light that falls on it.

Debussy (see on) adapted this impressionistic approach to music and he had to create his own rules of harmony and form to do so. This was a remarkable achievement. Ravel was also an Impressionist composer, but otherwise no one has really continued with Debussy's method.

CLAUDE DEBUSSY 1862-1918

Debussy was born in Paris and he spent most of his life in that city. At the age of twelve, he entered the *Paris Conservatoire.* Later he won its highest award, the *Prix de Roma,* as the outstanding student of the year. This gave him a scholarship to study in Rome for three years. On finishing this course, he went to Moscow, before settling in Paris as composer and journalist. When he was thirty-two, the performance of *L'Apres midi d'un Faune* scored his first success in the **Impressionist** style. His music met with wide acclaim but, at the height of his career, ill-health struck and a long decline began, leading to his death, from cancer. During his last years, his spirits and his inspiration increasingly failed.

Debussy was a **rebel against both classical and romantic styles.** He created his own rules of music and wrote in a very **personal** style. His music has a **dream-like quality. Images in sound** dissolve before their meaning is clear. His special sound is the result of several new techniques:

(i) Use of the **Whole Tone Scale** (C D E F♯G♯A♯). With all the intervals equal there is little feeling of tonality. He also used the **Pentatonic Scale** (5 note scale *e.g.* C D E G A).

(ii) He used only **fragments of melody,** rarely four-bar phrases. But the **harmony** and **texture** is as important as the melody.

(iii) **Rhythm** is more **flexible** than before. There are changing time signatures within a piece and, often, conflicting rhythm patterns are heard **(Polyrhythm).**

(iv) **Novel harmony,** due to the use of harmonics, wide spacing of intervals and to the scales used.

(v) **Novel orchestration,** due to unusual combinations of instruments and use of special effects.

Debussy prepared the way for twentieth-century composers to explore all the possibilities of sound and not feel bound by the rules of textbooks.

Piano Music

Like Chopin, Debussy turned his knowledge of the mechanics of the piano to his own advantage. He required the pianist to use his **feet** as carefully as his **fingers,** to produce **melting changes of harmony.** Sometimes a final chord may be held on the damper pedal long after it has been struck; if one listens carefully, the **overtones** are heard swelling and rippling in new patterns of sound. Many people come to know Debussy through his piano works. They are easy to listen to and often have helpful titles like: *La mer (The Sea); La fille aux cheveux de line (The Girl with the Flaxen Hair); Clair de lune (Moonlight); The Submerged Cathedral; Reflections in the Water; Arabesques; etc.*

Other Works

Piano *Estampes; Images; Children's Corner; Preludes; Etudes*
Orchestra *Three Nocturnes*
Opera *Pelléas and Mélisande*
Also Songs and String Quartet

GUSTAV MAHLER 1860-1911

An Austrian composer, Mahler is known for his fine **songs** and **song-cycles.** *Das Lied von der Erde (The Song of the Earth)* is a symphony for voice and orchestra. His **ten symphonies** are very **long** and very **profound.** It is only in recent times that his work has gained widespread recognition.

EDWARD ELGAR 1857-1934

The most British of composers, Elgar's music is **plain** and **noble.** The *Pomp and Circumstance Marches* were written for royal occasions. The *Enigma Variations* is his best known work. Each variation is a musical portrait of one of his friends. The 'enigma' or riddle was intended for his friends to recognise themselves in the music (*cf.* Variation Form). The *ninth variation* is solemn and patriotic and is often heard on solemn state occasions.

Other Works

Oratorio *The Dream of Gerontius*
Concertos *Violin; Concerto; Concerts*

RICHARD STRAUSS 1864-1949

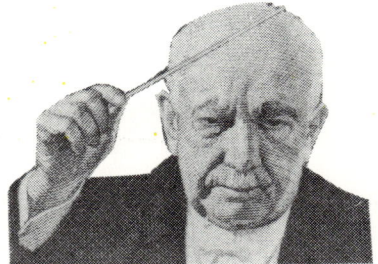

An Austrian composer and conductor who was an expert on Wagner, Strauss' own music was controversial for its **advanced harmony** and **heavy orchestration.** His opera, songs and **Tone Poems** are very popular. The Tone Poem *Till Eulenspiegal,* is based on the story of a practical joker. One humerous passage, for instance, describes in sound how *Till* charged through the market place, upsetting the stalls and sending pots and pans flying.

Works

Opera *Der Rosenkavalier* and fourteen others.
Symphonies and Tone Poems (12) *Don Juan; Don Quixote; Till Eulenspiegel; Tapiola*

MAURICE RAVEL 1875-1937

Though a French composer, Ravel's music has a strong **Spanish flavour.** He was an Impressionist, but his music is more **melodic** than Debussy's. In his *Bolero,* the **rhythm** is more important than the scrap of melody that runs through.

Other Works

Rhapsodie Espagnole
Pavan for a Departed Infant
Mother Goose Suite
Daphnis and Chloë (Impressionistic ballet music)

JEAN SIBELIUS 1865-1957

Finland was one of the first modern democratic countries to foster art using public funds. Before 1900, the government had given Sibelius a grant for life, which enabled him to achieve an international reputation and do pioneering work in recordings. It is said that European concern for the well-being of Finland was mainly the result of Sibelius' music. His music is strongly **nationalistic.** *Finlandia,* one of the most patriotic pieces of music ever written, reflects the long hard winter and the short brilliant summer of that country.

Other Works
Violin Concerto; Valse Triste; Piano works and songs

6 – Futuristic Music

Pablo Picasso

Musiciens aux Masques

(courtesy of the Philadelphia Museum of Art: A.E. Gallatin Collection)

FUTURISTIC MUSIC

As in the past, composers continue to break new ground. Many avoid the diatonic scales and use note-series of their own making and rules of harmony to go with them **(atonal** music and **serialism). Surprise, uncertainty** and **harshness** are featured. Orchestral instruments are no longer the only sources of musical sound; the human voice, traffic or machinery may be included and the orchestral instruments themselves are made to produce unexpected noises. Piano composers like John Cage attack the piano strings with wire brushes and drumsticks. Electronic instruments and the computer are brought to the concert platform. In what is called 'Now' music, players may improvise, the audience may participate and no one knows what may happen. Staff notation no longer suffices for notating such musical events and new systems of notation have been devised:

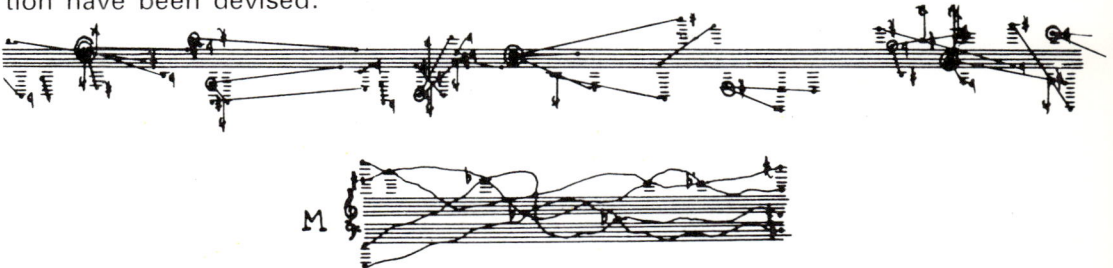

From the ms. of John Cage's concerto for piano and orchestra

In an age of change, it is not surprising that music should keep pace with the world, just as it has always done. Good music is no longer the preserve of a rich minority, it is there for all who wish to enjoy it. The barriers between classical, folk, pop and rock need no longer exist. Gerswin's *Rhapsody in Blue* may be enjoyed as much by a jazz fan as by a Chopin enthusiast.

ARNOLD SCHONBERG 1874-1951

Born in Vienna, to a Jewish family, Schonberg developed **atonal** music and wrote important text books on his theories. His music, often **harsh** and **dissonant,** was thought to be a fraud by early critics, but it opened up many new pathways for modern composers. Schonberg taught in Berlin, but fled from Nazi Germany to the U.S., where he lived until his death. He is best known for his opera *Moses and Aaron,* and for his orchestral piece, *A Survivor from Warsaw.*

BELA BARTOK 1881-1945

Hungarian born, Bartok collected thousands of folk tunes (which had little connection with the sentimental gipsy tunes used by Brahms and Liszt as folk music.) In his music, these are **dissonant** and have **vigorous** and even **brutal rhythms.** Bartok's musical efforts were failures and he lived in dire poverty. But, within a few months of his death, his music 'caught on'. He is now given an honoured place among great modern composers. His piano writings are in **classical forms** but use the **twelve-note scale.**

IGOR STRAVINGSKY 1882-1971

A Russian composer who enjoyed two careers in his lifetime, Stravingsky is best known for his ballet music. At the first performance of *The Rite of Spring* (Paris, 1913), the audience was shocked by what was seen and heard. In the music, Stravingsky had allowed **rhythm** to **take over** from **melody,** and the audience regarded the experiment as barbaric.

In 1937, Stravingsky went to live in America, but he continued to tour the world as conductor, until he was well over eighty. His later music is **neo-classical** - he used old forms and keys with great success. Now, people find it hard to decide whether he was greatest as a 'barbaric' or as a classical composer. His works include the ballets *Firebird* and *Petrushka,* and the opera *The Rake's Progress.*

KARL ORFF 1895-1982

Born in Munich, where he taught music, Orff was interested in involving amateurs and young people in music. His arrangements for percussion bands make music learning easy and enjoyable for children.

DIMITRY SHOSTAKOVICH 1906-1975

A product of Communist Russia, Shostakovich's music often comments on his country's troubled history *(e.g.* the *Leningrad Symphony).* The government could never make up its mind about his music. He was classified officially as both a 'dissident' and a 'hero' many times during his career. In latter years he received world wide acclaim, getting a warm welcome wherever he went.

Works

These include Nine Symphonies; the opera *Lady Macbeth of Mtsensk;* choral, piano and music for films

BENJAMIN BRITTEN 1913-1976

A leading British composer and promoter of music, Britten wrote opera very successfully in English. *The Turning of the Screw* is a spine-chilling music-drama in which the vocal line is close to speech. *Peter Grimes* is another popular opera. *The Young Persons' Guide to the Orchestra* was written to explain the instruments of the orchestra to aspiring musicians.

KARLHEINZ STOCKHAUSEN b. 1928

One of the best known names in contemporary music, this German teacher and composer uses the **twelve-note scale** and other sounds, besides those of musical instruments. **Improvisation** and **audience participation** form part of his music. He travels widely to conduct his own works.

RTE MUSIC DIARY 1982

JANUARY

Tuesday 12th
RTE Symphony Orchestra as part
of the Dublin Festival of Twentieth
Century Music.

Stockhausen: *Inori*
Conducted by Karlheinz Stockhausen

From the National Concert Hall's programme, January 1982, when Stockausen was billed to conduct his own work 'Inori'. The performance was cancelled, however, due to a sudden and unrelenting fall of snow which almost paralysed the city. Recordings of Stockhausen's music were played in the Concert Hall for the brave souls who turned up for the cancelled event.

Exercise

Using newspapers, *R.T.E. Guide, etc.* find out what musical works have been performed or broadcast during the past week. List the composers represented and gather some information about one of them.

7 —Irish Music

FOLK MUSIC

Features of Traditional Irish Folk Music include:

1. The use of **modes** (scales other than the diatonic major and minor). Remembering the monastic tradition in Ireland, it is no surprise that the modes used in Plainchant found their way into folksong.
2. The **plagal cadence** is often used, also as in plainchant.
3. **Gap scales** are often found, which omit certain degrees of the scale *e.g.* ommission of the 4th and 7th (Pentatonic).
4. Tunes may have a **very wide range.** This can make them very difficult for an untrained singer.
5. In the traditional style of singing, known as **sean nós,** the unaccompanied singer improvises freely on the melody.

Kinds of folk song

Love songs (Geantraí): They are about tragic love more often than happiness. The melodies match the words neatly in songs like *Úna Bhán; Eileen a Rún* and *An Draighnean Donn.*

Lullabies (Suantraí): Simple rocking tunes, as found in many countries: *e.g. Seothín Seo; Dilín Ó Deamhas.*

Laments (Caoine/Goltraí): The themes may be of death, emigration or eviction; *e.g. Caoine Cill Cais; Anach Cuain: Bán Chnoic Eireann Ó.*

Religious: When the religion of the native Irish (Catholicism) was "outlawed" during the Penal Days, they brought prayers into their daily lives through songs like *Aithrí Sheanín de Hóra* and *Caoine na Maighdine.*

Work Songs: These had strong rhythms to accompany certain tasks, *e.g. Ding Dong Dedero* for the forge and *Luibín Ó Lú* for spinning.

There were also **humourous songs; carols** and **boat songs** were scarce, an exception being the traditional carol singing in Kilmore, Co. Wexford.

Folk Dances

Spreading from England and Scotland since the Plantations, dancing was taught by travelling dance teachers, who were held in the same high respect as were the travelling scholars. In contrast with the rough living conditions in the country, Irish folk dances are **light, graceful** and **dignified.**

Young Irish dancers
(courtesy of Comhaltas Ceoltóirí Éireann)

Popular dances

Jig: In $\frac{6}{8}$ and $\frac{9}{8}$ time. A fast flowing step dance.

Reel: In $\frac{2}{4}$ or $\frac{4}{4}$ time. Fast and smooth with energetic steps.

Hornpipe: In $\frac{4}{4}$ time. Very rhythmical with complicated steps.

(Such tunes are often played with a dotted rhythm ♩. ♪ ♩. ♪ etc.)

Figure dances: These are danced by groups of people. The set movements are more important than the steps.

HARPS AND HARPERS

The harp was well known in ancient civilizations, but the Irish adopted it as a national emblem. It first appeared on Irish coinage a thousand years ago, and the *United Irishmen* put it on their flag for Ireland. Throughout the Middle Ages, bards were treated as honoured guests in the houses of the titled. Before visiting a patron, they would compose a song in his honour and like the *Troubadours* of Europe, they could compose verses suited to any occasion. They also recited sagas, to harp accompaniment, to pass away the long nights.

Turlough O'Carolan
(courtesy of The National Library of Ireland)

The earliest known harpers were **Rory Dall O'Cathain** from Derry and **Carroll O'-Daly** from Wexford. Both lived around 1600. **Turlough O'Carolan** (1670-1738) is the best known harper, however. A versatile and well-educated musician, he composed in the European style, as well as in the Gaelic tradition. About two hundred of his compositions are preserved. Born in Co. Meath, he suffered, as a boy, from small-pox and became blind as a result. He trained in music, at twenty-one setting out on horseback with a travelling companion to make his living as a harper. His skill was so great that he found the same welcome in the Anglo-Irish homes of the Pale as in the strongholds of the Gaelic chieftans. Dean Swift, among others, had a high regard for him.

Dublin was one of the cultural centres of Europe at this time. Carolan enjoyed there the best European music and his own was not thought inferior. He was particularly fond of Corelli's music, and work's like *Carolan's Concerto* sound more like the work of an Italian musician than of an Irish harper:

Belfast Harp Festival: 1792

The Society for the Preservation of Irish Poetry and Harp Music was founded in Belfast, in 1792. The political movement *The United Irishmen,* founded in the same year, shared some aims and some members with this cultural society. Henry Joy Mac-Cracken, who died in the 1798 rebellion, and others, decided to organise a **National Harp Festival** to revive interest in Irish music. Ten practising harpers, aged from 70 to 97, played at the festival. For four days they went through their repertoire, while **Edward Bunting** wrote down their music and described their playing styles. The most interesting player was **Dennis Hempson** (1695-1807), who was a greater virtuoso than Carolan. Hempson played with his fingernails, which he had allowed to grow to a great length. This gave a loud metalic quality to his playing. Hempson had had quite a reputation in both Ireland and England for the variety of effects which he had mastered. Although the old man of the festival, at ninty-seven years, Hempson was far from retiring. His career continued for a further fifteen years until his death at the astonishing age of 112.

This ambitious festival did not revive the bardic tradition. Indeed what was intended as a beginning was, in fact, a farewell. But, had it not taken place, little knowledge of the harping tradition would now be available.

IRISH MUSIC IN PRINT

Information is scanty about Ireland's musical past. Folk music is rarely written down and it can be forgotten when there are substantial social changes, as happened in Ireland in the ninteenth century. During this period people took traditional music for granted, and few realised that it was in danger of becoming extinct. Fortunately, some individuals began to collect and record this music which had survived orally for over a thousand years. These **collectors** of folk-music, between them, account for over 10,000 tunes which might otherwise have been lost.

The first **written** example of an Irish folk-tune is found in *William Ballet's Lute Book* (1600), which is kept in Dublin University. It is titled *Callino*. To an Irish ear, this easily becomes *'Cailín o cois tSuire me'*. This tune is mentioned by Shakespeare and is used later for the ballad *The Croppy Boy*. The earliest complete book of Irish airs was produced in 1726 by **John and William Neale.** The next significant publication was that of **Bunting** in 1809. An account of his work and that of other important ninteenth-century collectors follows.

Folk Music Collectors

EDWARD BUNTING 1773-1843

As an eighteen year old organist, Bunting was engaged to notate the music played at the **Belfast Harp Festival.** The notebook he used is still preserved. What began as only a job became Bunting's mission in life. He set out in an attempt to rescue the music that he realised was on the point of extinction. Bunting was the first collector to tackle the problem of saving folk-music in a scientific way. His collections include **commentaries** and valuable **background information.** He published *The Ancient Music of Ireland* in three volumes.

```
 66  airs, heard at the Belfast Harp Festival (pub. 1796)
 77  airs, which he collected in Munster and Connaught (1809)
143  further airs (1840)
```

HENRY HUDSON 1798-1889

A Dublin doctor, who developed a passion for Irish music, Hudson learned Irish and, while doing so, copied hundreds of tunes from his teacher. Later on, as editor of a cultural journal, *The Citizen,* he published many of these tunes. To prove a point, he began to include his own compositions as 'traditional' airs. It was an unworthy trick, and as a result, his M.S. collection, of over 800 airs, is treated by experts with some suspicion.

GEORGE PETRIE 1798-1866

Painter, antiquarian and scholar, Petrie's job with the *Ordnance Survey* took him all over the country, and he wrote down the music of the places he visited. Assisted by the Irish scholar, Eugene O'Curry, he published *The Ancient Music of Ireland,* in 1855. This book is an example of how folk music should be recorded. It classifies the songs and says where they were discovered. *The Derry Air,* one of the most remarkable of all melodies, is first seen in this collection. In 1857, he and O'Curry ventured to the Aran Islands on a study expedition. In his lifetime, Petrie collected thousands of tunes and provided material for several publications after his death. *A Complete Petrie Collection* was edited by Charles Stanford, in 1905.

WILLIAM FORDE 1795-1850

A Cork-based musician, Forde was expert in both classical music and in the folk music of many countries. He collected countless Irish airs and, in 1845, proposed a scholarly publication of 4,000 airs. It was to be a new approach, giving all the available versions of each air, together with commentaries. He failed to raise the 250 guineas needed for the project, however, and he left the country for good.

JOHN PIGOT 1822-1871

Son of a prominant lawyer, Pigot joined the Young Ireland movement in 1841 and became a close friend of Thomas Davis. He aroused widespread interest in folk music through articles published in *The Nation.* His collected airs are preserved by the *Royal Irish Academy.*

JAMES GOODMAN 1828-1896

Born near Dingle, Goodman was rector of a parish in Kerry and Professor of Irish in Dublin University. A keen piper himself, he collected about 2,000 unknown airs. Bridging the gap between Protestants and Catholics, this unusual parson was as happy playing for the humble of his parish as for the university professors.

PATRICK WESTON JOYCE 1827-1914

Joyce was a Limerick man who came to live in Dublin. Petrie was impressed by his knowledge of folk music and persuaded him to write down the Limerick airs that he remembered. After Petrie's death, he published about a hundred airs under the title *Ancient Music of Ireland* (1873). In 1909 he published *Old Irish Music and Songs,* a collection of 842 airs taken from the unpublished works of Pigot and Forde. When he died, he was working on a third volume of over 900 airs.

JAMES O'NEILL

O'Neill was a member of the Chigago police force, who collected about 2,000 tunes from Irish emigrants in America. He published the collection in 1903. It is still a popular source book for traditional players.

ANGLO-IRISH MUSIC

During the ninteenth century, the language and music of the many settlers who came to Ireland, filtered through the country. Thousands of Irish labourers migrated seasonally, to Scotland and England, bringing back the music which they heard there. New words were often attached to old melodies. Such ballads were distributed throughout the country in **Broadsheet** form. Sold at fairs and gatherings they stirred the hearts of the peasantry with heady thoughts of freedom and rebellion, *e.g. Robert Emmet; The Wearing of the Green; A Nation Once Again; Shan Van Bhocht; The Boys of Wexford.*

Besides patriotic themes, the broadsheets dealt with topics of local interest. They are a source of social history in that they give a glimpse of life as it was for the ordinary person *'My Bonny Boy',* for instance, dating from before the Famine, tells of poor conditions, early marriage and untimely death.

Moore's Melodies give a **romantic** view of Ireland, aimed at the more educated classes of Moore's time. Later, music-hall composers spread their image of Ireland through England and America. They paint a blissful picture of life in rural Ireland and they often express the feelings of the emigrant recalling his home and the loved ones left forever *(The Kerry Dances; The Low-Backed Car; The Irish Emigrant).* Such songs have enjoyed enormous popularity.

IRISH NAMES IN MUSICAL HISTORY

John Egan: Dublin instrument maker. Around 1800 he developed a good pedal harp and improved the bagpipes.

John and William Neale: Dublin's first music publishers. In 1726 they published *A Book of Irish Tunes* and *A Collection of Irish and Scotch Tunes.* For the next century the music publishing business was a big industry in Dublin. The laws of Copyright did not extend to Ireland and many English publishing houses opened branches in Dublin, allowing them to publish 'pirated' material in safety. The Neales also promoted musical entertainments. They built the *Musick Hall* in 1741 and netted the première of Handel's *Messiah* the following year.

MICHAEL KELLY 1762-1826

Irish tenor, actor and composer of European fame, Kelly studied singing and piano in Dublin until he was eighteen, then left for training in Naples. He worked at the Court in Vienna for four years where he was friend and pupil of Mozart. He sang in the first performance of *The Marriage of Figaro* (1786). Settling in London, he was, in turn, theatre manager, music shop owner and wine importer. He continued to sing and produce his own works in England and Ireland. There was a suspicion that he had passed off some of Mozart's work as his own, and a well known writer, Sheridan, suggested that the sign over his shop should read:

```
┌─────────────────────────────────┐
│                                 │
│      Composer of Wines          │
│                                 │
│              and                │
│                                 │
│      Importer of Music          │
│                                 │
└─────────────────────────────────┘
```

THOMAS MOORE 1779-1852

A fine singer and the best paid poet of his day, Moore romanticised Irish history in **good poems neatly joined to old Irish airs.** His songs are **art-songs** rather than folk songs because he changed the airs to regular forms. He was a celebrity in the drawing rooms of Ireland and England. He used Bunting's collections, without permission, and this caused bad blood between the two. Popular history has added insult to injury by referring to these songs as *Moore's Melodies.* Where Bunting had done the spadework, Moore has reaped the harvest. Some of Moore's best known songs are:

Let Erin Remember the Days of Old
The Harp that Once through Tara's Halls
At the Mid Hour of Night
The Meeting of the Waters

JOHN FIELD 1782-1837

Music was "whipped" into young Field by his father and grandfather, both out-standing musicians. Like Mozart, he was paraded before the public as a prodigy when he was eight. At eleven he went to London to study under Clementi, the pianist and piano-maker. Field often demonstrated the pianos in Clementi's showroom. Haydn heard him playing and predicted a great future for him. In 1802, Clementi took him to St. Petersburg on a sales trip, and there Field decided to stay. Clementi had been a hard and miserly master and Field took his revenge by throwing a hugh party in the most expensive hotel and leaving the account for Clementi to settle.

In St. Petersburg, Field became very popular with the nobility and was spoiled by them. He toured Europe as a virtuoso pianist and gained a high reputation for his play-ing. His Concertos and Nocturnes were also very popular. He devised the **Nocturne form** and Chopin copied this form and style from him. His biggest contribution to music was his mastery of the **singing style for piano.**

MICHAEL BALFE 1808-1870

Dublin born, Balfe was both opera composer and singer. With his wife as leading lady, he enjoyed comfortable success, producing his operas in the leading cities of Europe. When he had saved enough money, he abandoned the pressures of musical life and spent the rest of his days as a gentleman farmer. Two of his works have stood the test of time, *The Bohemian Girl* and *The Rose of Castille.*

VINCENT WALLACE 1812-1865

Waterford born composer Wallace's reputation rests on his popular opera *Maritana.* It shows a great gift for lyrical melody. Undoubtedly, of all Irish musicians, Wallace was the one whose fame spread furthest in his lifetime. A man of great charm, he was given a gift of two hundred sheep for a concert in Australia. In New Zealand, he was captured by natives, and would have been killed but for a romantic rescue by the chief's daughter. He was treated with high honours in India, Mexico and the United States. After an adventurous ten years, he returned to Europe, where his operas were outstanding successes. He produced a vast amount of music, little of which is now played.

JOHN COUNT MacCORMACK

1884-1945

A Tenor from Athlone, with a voice of unsurpassed beauty, MacCormack was trained in Dublin and Italy. He achieved amazing technical perfection. His power of expression was such that he could 'sell' the most difficult music even to uneducated listeners, and his singing of the simple music of the people won the hearts of several generations.

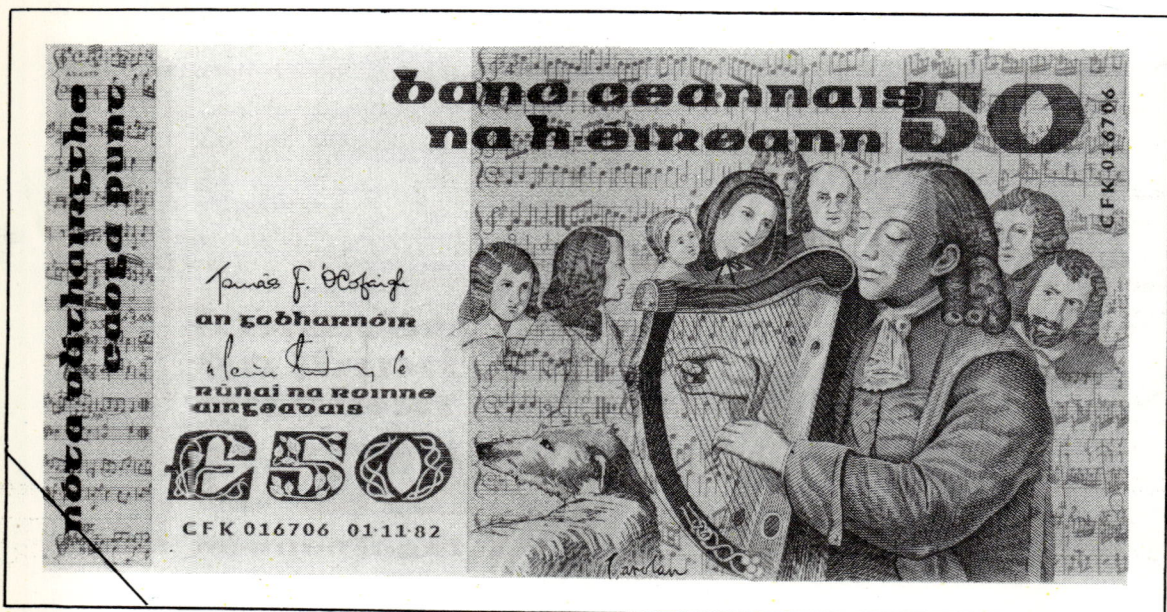

£50 note featuring Irish musicianship as its theme. Do you recognise the harpist?

Find Out!

Using the Ordnance Survey Street Map of Dublin find the area (south side) where the streets are all named after various Irish musicians. Use the street index, attached to the map, as a guide, and it you get really lost, ask your Geography teacher to lend a hand!

MUSIC IN IRELAND TODAY

Tastes have changed and the gap between 'serious' and popular music has narrowed. Light entertainers now bring the same level of professionalism to their work as was always expected from 'serious' performers. It is now acceptable to see a national orchestra share a platform with traditional or pop musicians. Education is creating an informed public, which will hopefully support and enjoy the many branches of music. A typical month's programme of the *National Concert Hall* shows that there is a great variety of fun and pleasure possible under the general heading 'Musical Events'.

AN CEOLÁRAS NÁISIÚNTA
THE NATIONAL CONCERT HALL
Earlsfort Terrace, Dublin 2 Tel: (01) 711888

SEPTEMBER EVENTS

Sat SEPT 4th	**Clannad** £2.50, £4.50, £5.50.
Wed SEPT 8th	**RTE Symphony Orchestra**, Conductor: **Albert Rosen**, Soloist: **Lynda Byrne** (piano) £2.00, £3.00.
Thurs SEPT 9th	**Young Irish Artists Benefit Concert.**
Fri SEPT 10th	**Wicklow Choral Society, New Irish Chamber Orchestra**, Conductor: John Beckett (Haydn 250th Anniversary Concert), £1.50, £3.00, £4.00.
Sat SEPT 11th	**Preservation Hall Jazz Band** £3.50, £4.50, £5.50, £6.50.
Sun SEPT 12th	**Preservation Hall Jazz Band** £3.50, £4.50, £5.50, £6.50.
Tues SEPT 14th	**RTE Singers** £2.00.
Wed SEPT 15th	**RTE Symphony Orchestra**, Conductor: **Colman Pearce**, Soloist: **Richard Markson** (cello) £2.00, £3.00.
Thurs SEPT 16th	**Oscar Peterson** £5.00, £7.50, £10.00, £12.50.
Fri SEPT 17th	**Oscar Peterson** £5.00, £7.50, £10.00, £12.50.
Sat SEPT 18th	**Giuseppe di Stefano** (tenor), **Monika Curth** (soprano), **Enrico di Mori** (piano), (In aid of St. Luke's Hospital) £6.00, £12.00, £18.00.
Sun SEPT 19th	3 p.m.–5 p.m.: Lecture on John McCormack by **Fr. Sydney McEwan** £1.50, 8 p.m. **John McCormack Commemoration Concert** £2.00, £3.00.
Wed SEPT 22nd	**RTE Symphony Concert**, Conductor: **Eimear O Broin**, Soloist: **Paul Crossley** (piano) £2.00, £3.00.
Thurs SEPT 23rd	**Dutch Swing College Band** £3.00, £4.00, £5.00, £6.00.
Sun SEPT 26th	**New Irish Chamber Orchestra** £2.00, £3.00, £4.00.
Wed SEPT 29th	**RTE Symphony Orchestra**, Subscription Concert, Soloist: **Leon Bates** (piano), Conductor: **Stephen Gunzenhauser**, £2.00, £3.00, £4.00, £5.00

Even if we regard the music trade as commercial industry, all kinds of Irish musicians, by their foreign tours and by their recordings, 'sell' not only their records but Ireland itself to the outside world. This brings revenue and good-will to the country.

While music has largely been a 'spectator sport' in the past, more and more people now want to involve themselves in active music-making. A short list of some institutions and activities presently in vogue suggests that music can be at once entertainment, social activity and an absorbing hobby for young and old alike.

State Sponsored: Two R.T.E. orchestras; The R.T.E. Singers and Cork-based String Quartet.

Arts Council: This body sponsors various musical activities.

Comhaltas Ceoltóirí Eireann: Promotes traditional music, having many branches throughout the country. It runs Fleadh Ceoil.

Siamsa: Tralee based traditional entertainment.

Festivals of Music: Wexford, Waterford, Kilkenny, Gorey, Belfast, Dublin.

Feiseanna: Dublin, Cork, Limerick, Sligo, Arklow.

Amateur Musical Societies: In most towns throughout the country many are members of the *Association of Irish Musical Societies (AIMS)*.

Amateur and professional orchestras: In Dublin and some of the bigger towns.

Bands, Choirs and Choral Societies: In almost every part of the country.

Music Association of Ireland (M.A.I.): This body promotes musical involvement throughout the country.

Slógadh: This body brings together young people from all over the country, in various regional competitions, run completely through Irish, culminating in finals week held each year in a different county.

A Set Dance group performing at Fleadh Cheoil na hÉireann
(courtesy of Comhaltas Ceoltóirí Éireann)

8 — Musical Instruments and the Orchestra

Musical sounds may be produced by beating, plucking, bowing or blowing.

1. Beating: These instruments go back to primitive man and, in some parts of the world, prehistoric instruments are still known. **Drums** were fashioned from hollowed tree trunks and gourds. The tightly stretched skin vibrates when beaten and the hollow body acts as **resonator.** Drums were used for dancing, accompaniment and communication.

The **Xylophone,** in its primitive form — the **Marimba** — is still known in Mexico. It was made from logs of different lengths laid over a pit and beaten with sticks. **Wood blocks, notched stick, castenets** and many other wooden percussion instruments have a very long history. **Gongs, cymbals** and **bells** are mentioned many times in the Bible. The bell, thought to drive away evil spirits, was always associated with funerals and still has great religious meaning.

2. Plucking: A tight string which is plucked, vibrates and produces a musical note. **Guitar, harp** and **lute** are plucked by fingers or plectrum. The **harpsichord** strings are plucked by plectra worked from a keyboard.

Forerunners of the guitar and banjo, **lutes** were the most popular of instruments by 1600, chiefly because anyone could learn to play simple music on them, or use them to accompany singing. The **Therabo** was the most advanced lute, having about sixteen strings, and was as much in demand as was the piano later on.

What the lute was to England and France however, the **harp** was to Ireland. The harp has a string for every note of the major scale. By means of pedals the **Concert Harp** can be retuned instantly to any other scale. It has a range of about six octaves and its sound quality is very special. Harp glissandos are especially effective.

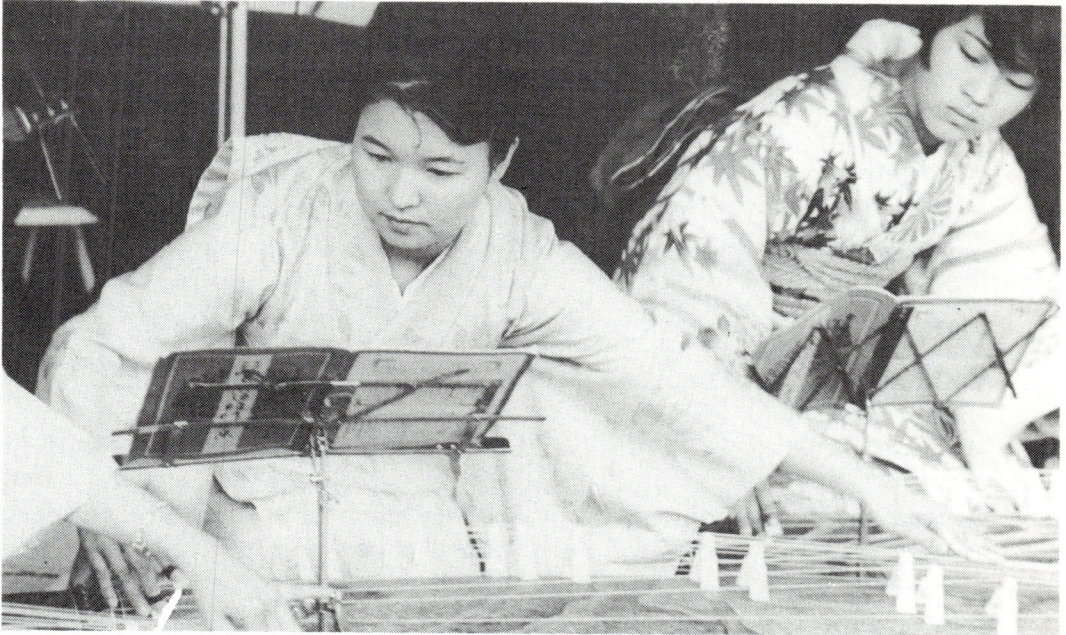

An unusual and ancient plucking instrument, the Japanese Koto, said to have taken its shape from that of a crouching dragon. (courtesy of the Embassy of Japan)

3. Bowing Instruments: Viols were bowed instruments of four or five strings. They were held downward on the lap or gripped between the knees of the player. The viols gradually gave way to the more versatile members of the violin family. Renaissance instrument-makers applied the new scientific knowledge of the period to producing instruments that threatened to surpass the beauty of the human voice in their sweetness of tone and range of expression. From the *Cremona* workshops of the **Amati** and **Stradivarii** families came stringed instruments that are still superb.

A 'chest' of viols (15th Cent.)

(Larousse)

Of all instruments, the bowed ones are considered to be most sensitive and expressive. Some factors which effect their sound quality are:

(i) **Where the bow is placed.** Near the bridge, it gives a loud brilliant tone; near the fingerboard, it is soft and mellow.

(ii) **Vibrato.** By shaking the hand in a special way each note is made to throb with a warm singing sound.

(iii) **Harmonics.** Produced by touching the string lightly at a **node** and bowing gently.

(iv) **Double stopping.** Two or three strings may be made to sound at the same time. In his cello and violin suites, Bach challenges the player to play two or three different tunes at the same time.

4. Blowing Instruments: The **Flute** and **Recorder,** as well as a host of reeded in-struments were well developed in the 17th century. Some woodwind instruments had a few keys but their compass was determined mainly by the stretch of the player's hand. Such instruments were the **Shawn; Bourbon; Hautboy (oboe); Crumhorn** and **Racket** (a cleverly made bass instrument sounding like a bassoon). During the 18th century the **keyed Flute; Oboe; Clarinet** and **Bassoon** superceded all other woodwind.

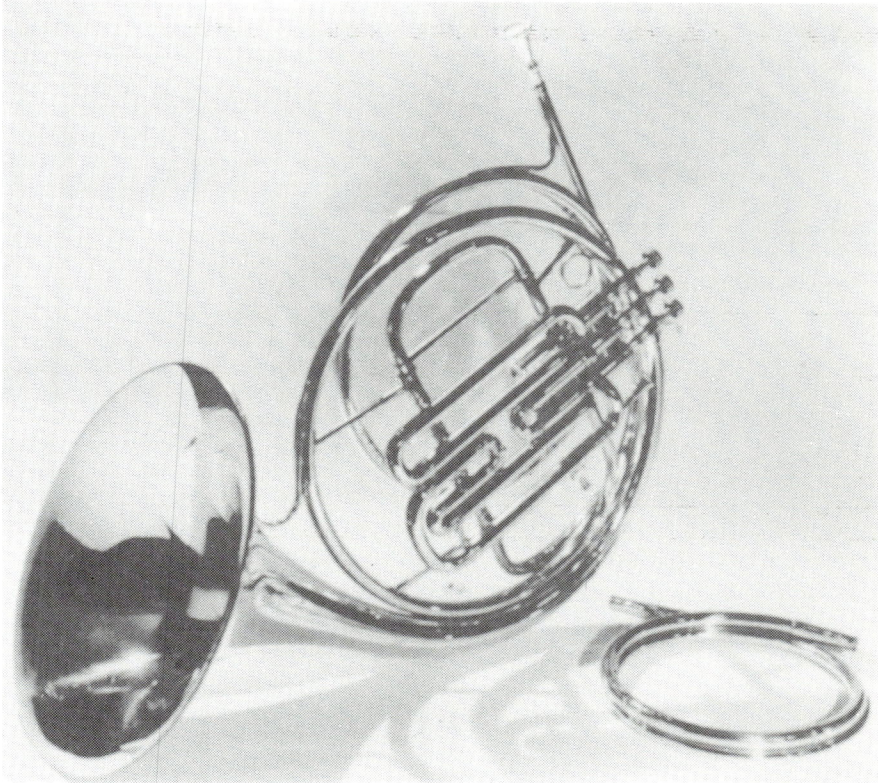

French Horn (Larousse)

In 1600, the brass instruments were still most at home on the battlefield and the hunting ground. The **Cornett** and **Trumpet** gradually crept 'indoors' and a strange selection of brass instruments were tried out in orchestras. It was not until the inven-tion of the **Valved Trumpet,** by Bluhmel, around 1830, that brass instruments were perfected. Despite their limitations, medieval instruments made a cheerful sound and interest has been revived in them in the 20th century.

Instrument-making in the 18th century. From the French 'Encyclopedie', 1767.
(courtesy of the British Library)

TIMBRE

The sound quality **(timbre)** of instruments varies with the **shape** of the body and the **material** from which it is made. This is why great skill is required in the construction of instruments and few can be mass-produced successfully. Changes of timbre may be demonstrated by sounding a tuning fork on different surfaces.

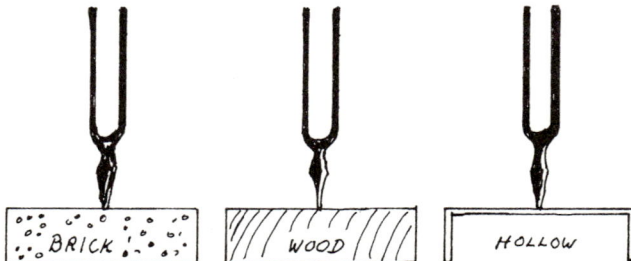

The timbre of a wind instrument depends mainly on the shape of its **bore** (inside) *e.g.*

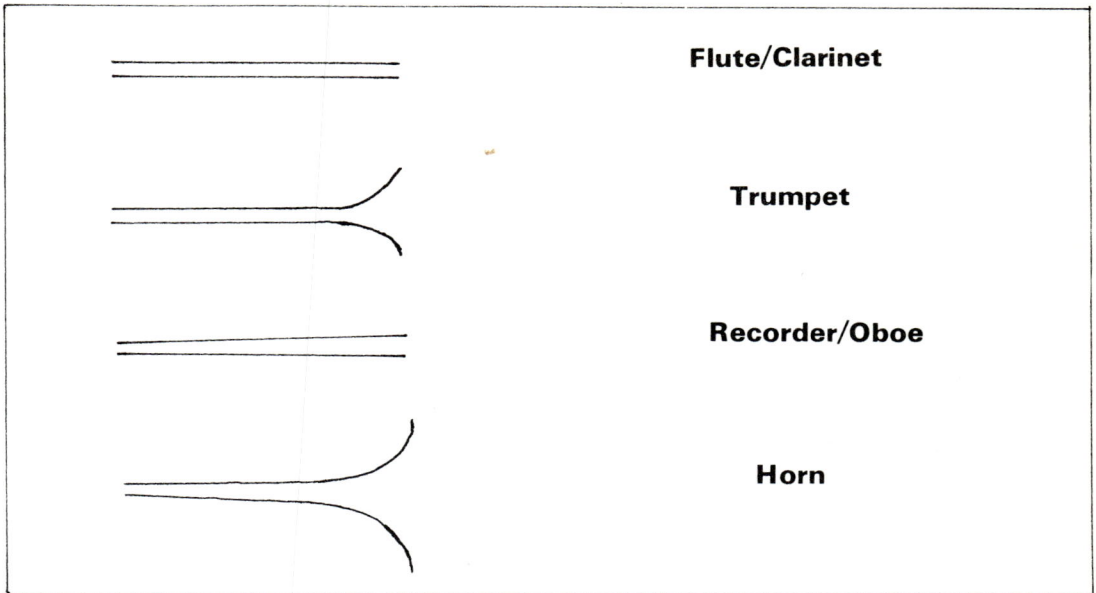

Flute/Clarinet

Trumpet

Recorder/Oboe

Horn

PITCH

The **pitch** of a stringed instrument depends on the **length, thickness** and **tension** of the string. **Pitch** is altered by shortening the string. This is done by stopping it with the fingers. The shorter the string, the higher the pitch. Plucked strings and the viols have a fretted fingerboard, while modern bowed instruments have a plain fingerboard.

The **pitch** of wind instruments depends on the volume of vibrating air. Shortening the tube will raise the pitch. The effective length of the tube may be altered by opening or closing holes in the side of it.

Example: A length of tube sounds the note D

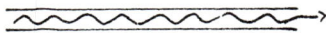

Half that length sounds the octave higher

With small instruments, the holes may be controlled by the fingers, but with longer ones, the holes are spaced beyond the stretch of the fingers. Keys are then used to reach the holes.

With brass instruments, the shape and tension of the player's lips alone can produce several notes of the harmonic series. **Valves** are now used to change the length of the tube and so produce a different set of harmonics. By using lips and valve, the brass player now has a full range of notes. The trombone uses a sliding valve to get the same effect.

OVERTONES

Because a string (or air-column) vibrates in parts as well as in full, several notes are produced at once. The main sound heard is the **fundamental** note, the lesser sounds heard are called **harmonics** or **overtones.** The harmonics are higher notes which are related mathematically to the fundamental note.

Pythagoras (Greece 600 B.C.) was the first to explain the mathematical nature of sound. He studied the complex movements of a vibrating string:

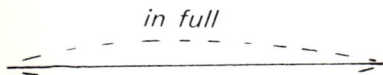

in full

vibrates in full giving fundamental note **(C).**

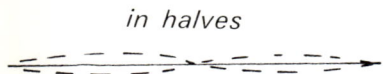

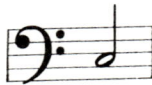

in halves

also vibrates in halves, first overtone **(C),** *(octave higher).*

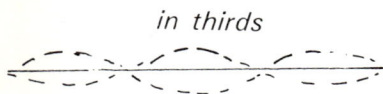

in thirds

also vibrates in thirds, second overtone **(G),** *(fifth higher).*

The series continues indefinitely in quarters, fifths, *etc*. The points where the vibrating sections of the string divide are called **nodes.** It is not always easy to hear the harmonics. A simple experiment is to strike a low note on the piano and listen carefully as the sound dies away. It is possible to hear the harmonics as the fundamental note fades. Brass and string players can pick out a single harmonic and cause it to sound clearly.

Harmonic series:

The Strings

The string family (all instruments played with a bow) consists of:

Violin	Strings tuned to G, D, A and E
Viola	Strings tuned to C, G, D and A
Violoncello (usually called 'cello)	Strings tuned to C, G, D and A
Double Bass (usually called Bass)	Strings tuned to E, A, D and G

The bow is itself a carefully made instrument. Much depends on its strength and balance.

Of all instruments, the strings are the most versatile, but they also demand the greatest skill from the player. String tone is the foundation of most orchestral textures. It can range from mellow to brilliant, from very quiet to very loud. The *VIOLIN* is the supreme solo and orchestral instrument. The VIOLA is heard less often as a solo instrument. It is often used to fill in the inner harmony in orchestration. The *CELLO* plays an important role in the bass line of harmony, but its wide compass and range of tone make it a prime solo instrument. The *BASSES* form a solid line of sound, on which the various orchestral textures are woven. The bass is a very big instrument needing a player with big hands. It is occasionally heard as a solo instrument and it can produce an unexpectedly sweet tone.

DOUBLE BASS

CELLO

VIOLA

The Woodwind

FLUTE

This is a very graceful and agile instrument with a velvety lower register and brilliant upper reaches. It is used for both light and serious music. The *PICCOLO* is a smaller flute. It sounds an octave higher than the concert flute.

OBOE

This is a **double reed** instrument with an incisive tone of nasal quality. Because it 'speaks' more slowly than other instruments, sustained melodies are characteristic of it. Because of its clear sound, other orchestral instruments take their tuning from the oboe.

The *COR ANGLAISE* is the bass version of the oboe. It has a rather sad sound, especially in the lower register. It is a **transposing instrument** which sounds a **fifth** lower than the written music.

CLARINET

This is a **single-reed** instrument, with a hollow sound in the lower register. It has a wide compass and is a good solo instrument. Of all the woodwind family, it has the greatest range of dynamics. **A transposing instrument,** clarinets in B♭ and A are most common now.

BASSOON

This is a **double-reed** instrument, which forms the bass of the woodwind section in the orchestra. Despite its size ($2\frac{1}{2}$ metre tube), the bassoon is agile in fast passages. It has an even tone throughout its compass and is a beautifully melodic instrument. In orchestration, it is often used to accompany a second woodwind instrument.

The *DOUBLE BASSOON* goes an octave lower than the normal bassoon.

COR ANGLAISE

OBOE

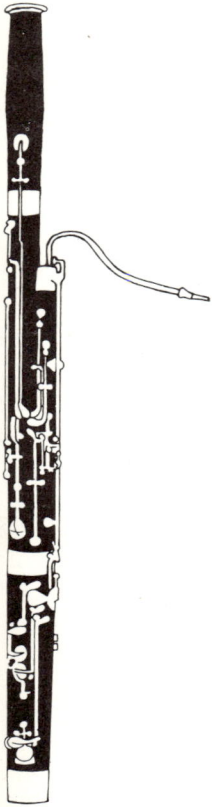

FLUTE

BASSOON   **OBOE**   **CLARINET** **FLUTE**

BASSOON

CLARINET

The Brass

TRUMPET

Trumpet tone is very brilliant in its higher register. Rapid passages and repeated notes are possible. An important solo instrument, it also gives sparkle to orchestral sound. The muted trumpet produces a very distinct effect. Of the many sized trumpets made, the one in B♭ is now most common **(transposing).**

FRENCH HORN

The French Horn tone is very mellow in soft music, so it is often included in woodwind ensembles. Its loud tone is very commanding. In orchestras, the horns fill in the middle harmonies, often with sustained notes. The horn in F is now most commonly used. By tradition, horn music is written without a key signature, but many modern writers do not follow this rule.   (A transposing instrument.)

TROMBONE

The length of tube in the Trombone is varied by means of a **slide-valve** which has seven positions. Each position produces a different fundemental and harmonic series. *Glissando* effects are possible and are often used for comedy effects. The trombone is loud and impressive. The modern orchestra uses two tenors and a bass trombone.

TUBA

Often the 'clown' of orchestra and bands because of its thick, 'floppy' sound. The tuba adds weight to accents and is associated with *'Oom-pa-pa'* rhythms. The **transposing** Tuba in F is now in common use.

Mutes are used to alter the sound of various Brass instruments.

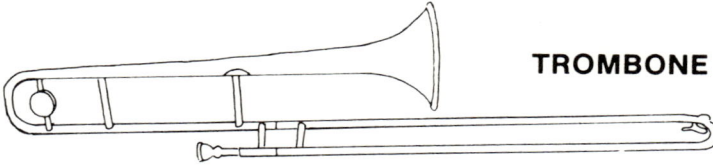

TROMBONE

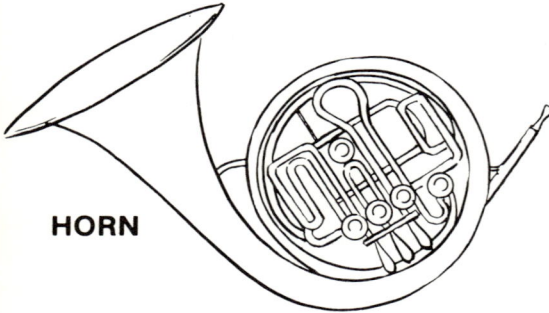

HORN

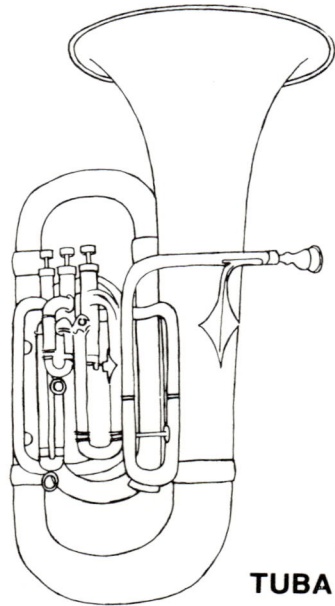

TUBA

TRUMPET

Percussion Instruments

Percussion instruments make their sound by being "struck". They include the Timpani (kettledrum), Bass Drum, Side Drum, Cymbals and Triangle. These drums are used to give a "roll" effect of continous sound or they may contribute to crescendo and diminuendo effects.

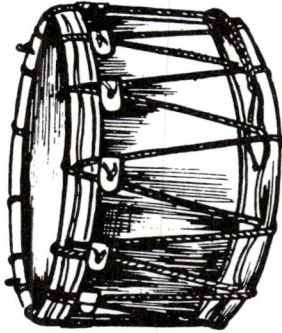

BASS DRUM

SIDE DRUM

TIMPANI

Resources to Illustrate the Use of Orchestral Instruments

General: Benjamin Britten, *Young Person's Guide to the Orchestra*
Prokofiev, *Peter and the Wolf*
Kodaly, *Hary Janos Suite* (for W.W. and Brass esp.)

STRINGS

Cello: Rossini, *William Tell Overture* (opening section)
Bass: Beethoven, *Symphony No. 5* (third movement)

WOODWIND

Piccolo: Tchaikowsky, *Nutcracker Suite* (Chinese Dance)
Flute: Recordings by James Galway
Oboe: Handel, *Oboe Concerto*
         Bach, *Suite in D* (Bar 50, first move.)
Cor Anglaise: Dvorak, *Symphony From the New World* (2nd. move.)
Clarinet: Mozart, *Clarinet Quintet*
Bassoon: Mozart, *Bassoon Concerto; Don Giovanni* (ghost scenes)
         Dukas, *The Sorcerer's Apprentice*

BRASS

Trumpet: Haydn, *Trumpet Concerto*
Muted Trumpets: Debussy, *Fêtes* (middle section)
Horn: Haydn, *Horn Concerto*
Trombone: Wagner, *Tannhauser Overture*
Tuba: Kleinsinger, *Tubby the Tuba*
         Mussorgsky, *Pictures from an Exhibition (Bydlo)*

PERCUSSION

Timpani: Rossini, *"William Tell" Overture.*

COMPASS OF INSTRUMENTS

Only an approximate idea of the compass can be given. The highest and lowest notes of most instruments will depend on the skill of the players. The table below also shows the notes to which strings are tuned:

THE ORCHESTRA

Medieval orchestras were groups of players who played a random selection of instruments. As instruments improved, people enjoyed making music together, playing the part-songs and dances already in existence. Stringed instruments were the core of the group. Flutes and oboes added colour to the sound and occasionally, brass and percussion instruments were borrowed from 'fife and tabour' bands to give punch to the sound. The **harpsichord player** was the leader of the group. His business was to keep the music in time and to fill in whatever was missing. His copy often contained no more that a **figured bass** *i.e.* a sketch of the harmonic scheme, and from this he improvised. Soon composers began to compose for certain groups of instruments, discovering that instruments had qualities different from the human voice. It was an experimental and an exciting time.

Haydn worked out a proper **orchestral balance** without the need for a keyboard instrument. His symphonies were written for the *Esterhazy Orchestra,* 23 strong, deployed as follows:

> Eleven violins along with pairs of — violas; cellos; double-basses; oboes; bassoons and horns.

The **clarinet** was given a place by Mozart, who was very fond of it. With Beethoven, the accepted balance became:

> 20/30 strings; with pairs of — flutes; oboes; clarinets; bassoons; trumpets; horns and trombones.

From Classical times, **timpani** of definite pitch were used. But Modern orchestras may field as many as six percussion players and a stronger brass section. The standard layout for a modern orchestra is:

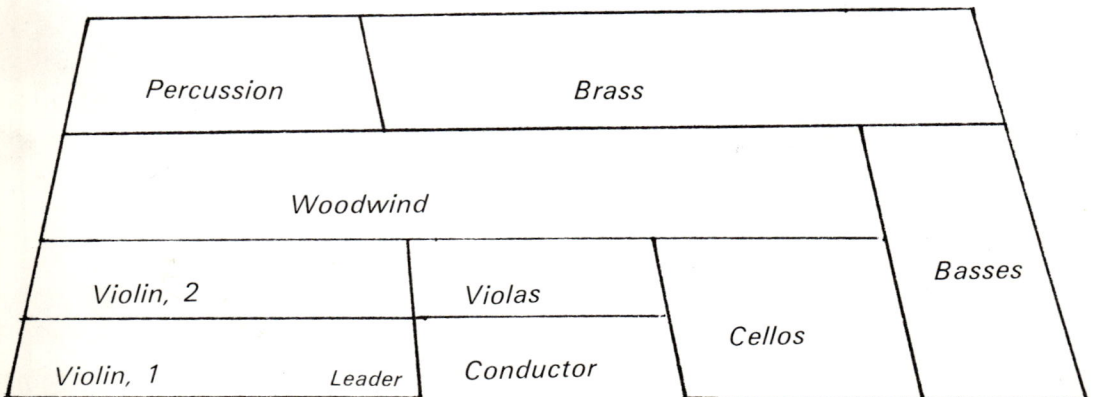

The symphony orchestra has **four** sections — **Woodwind, Brass, Percussion** and **Strings.** The diagram below shows the instruments of each section and how an orchestral score is laid out:

Section	Instruments	Number	Alternative Instruments	Score (All playing the keynote F)	
Woodwind	Flute	2	Piccolo	Fl.	
	Oboe	2	Cor Anglais	Ob.	
	Clarinet	2	Bass Clarinet	Clar. in A	
	Bassoon	2	Double Bassoon	Bass.	
Brass	French Horn	2		Hrn. in F	
	Trumpet	2		Tpt. in B♭	
	Trombone	3	Bass Trombone	Trom.	
	Tuba	1		Tuba in F	
Percussion	Timpani	1+	Celesta	Timp.	
	Cymbals		Snare Drum, etc		
	Bells				
String	Violin	30		Vln. 1	
	Viola	12		Vln. 2	
	Cello	10		Vla.	
	Bass	8		Cello & Bass	

Transposing Instruments

To make reading easier for the players, some instruments sound at a pitch below the written music. (This practice arose long ago when wind players used different sized instruments, depending on which keys they were required to play in.)

Examples of Transposing Instruments:

Instrument	Written music	Sounds	Difference
Trumpet in B flat			a tone lower
Clarinet in A			a minor third lower
Horn in F			a fifth lower

Exercise

  (i) Give an account of the origin of the Symphony Orchestra.
 (ii) Name the four sections of the modern orchestra and make a list of the instruments usually found in each section.
(iii) Make a list of the instruments that make up any one section of the orchestra. Give a description of each of those instruments.

Exploration

A useful project is to trace the changing **texture** and **balance** of the orchestra by comparing short excerpts from each period. A suggested listening guide follows:

Period	Watch out for
Medieval *Example:* any available recording	Shrill crisp sound quality from woodwind, reeded and flute family. Contrapunctual structure; tightly-knit texture.
Baroque *Example:* Bach — *Suite for Orchestra*	Uniform and rounded sound quality; strings dominate; occasional brass and the keyboard may be heard. Contrapunctual structure; every instrument is busy.
Classical *Example:* Haydn — *Trumpet Concerto*	Homophonic music; balanced four-bar phrases, texture is clear; with pleasant changes of sound colour; sudden louds and softs; strings dominant; but lots of colour from woodwind and brass.
Romantic *Example:* Beethoven — *5th Symphony* (opening)	Rich sounds of great depth; homophonic and expressive with changing moods; freedom and variety of melody; all instruments play vital roles.
Modern *Example:* Stravingsky — *Rite of Spring* (opening)	Excitement and tension from strong rhythm and abrupt melodies, very colourful sounds, from dark and muddy to brilliant. All sections of orchestra are hard worked, esp. brass and percussion.

THE ROLE OF THE CONDUCTOR

Stravinsky conducts

Orchestral playing started in the Middle Ages with democratic groups who came together for pleasure. The forces of a modern orchestra, however, are ruled by a conductor, who commands like a general on the field of battle. This change did not come about without a long and bitter struggle.

In the Middle Ages, the keyboard player was in charge. Often, he was the organiser of the group and provided the meeting-place. He beat time, and the other players followed his lead. He could improvise and generally keep the music going. But, during the Eighteenth Century, the keyboard was gradually dropped from the orchestra and redundant pianists conducted with a roll of music. The first violin also claimed the right of leadership, waving his bow to start the music and to egg the players on to greater efforts. As orchestras grew in size and music became more difficult, the need for a non-playing conductor was realised. But orchestral players did not surrender to the outsider easily. Early conductors always conducted facing the audience, with the result that if the players resented the presence of the conductor, the first violinist would beat time in opposition, and throw the music into confusion.

In the Romantic period, interpetation became one of the conductor's main duties. Beethoven is described by an eye witness as crouching behind his desk to indicate soft passages gradually rising with the crescendos, and bounding into the air to incite the orchestra to a deafening climax. Conductors like Mendelssohn and Berlioz put music before manners and faced the orchestra, so that by hands and looks they could remind the players of every shade of expression.

The familiar white *baton,* both a magic wand and a symbol of authority, becomes an instrument in the hands of a modern conductor. He plays on his orchestra as if it were a single instrument and he the only performer. Many conductors discard the baton and, almost as mime artists, using gestures of hand and expressions of face, unveil the hidden thoughts of the composer for players and audience.

Some famous conductors include:
Sir Thomas Beecham
Leonard Bernstein
Leopold Stokowsky
Arther Toscanini

KEYBOARD INSTRUMENTS

It was not until 1600 that keyboard instruments began to improve and develop rapidly. Early organ keyboards were a crude sets of levers, which had to be struck with the fist.

Clavichord, Spinet and **Virginals** were small keyboard instruments, sounded by either metal blades or feathers. They were quite small and played on a table. They had a simple direct-lever action.

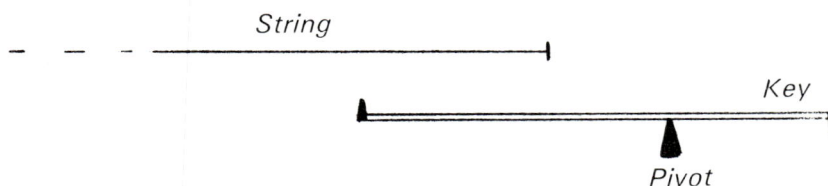

String

Key

Pivot

By 1750 the **Harpsichord** had reached its peak. The **wing-shaped cabinet and the reliable action** were examples of supreme craftsmanship. Having two or three keyboards and **stops** to change the tone, the harpsichord inspired great writing by the Baroque composers. But it had a **limited dynamic range** and **carrying power,** and its sound could become tiresome.

Tradition upholds the claim of Christofori of Padua to have made the first **Piano** in 1709. The importance of his invention is seen in its simple name — *Fortepiano, (loud soft).* Beyond changing the order of the words and shortening it to 'piano', no one has thought of a better name. For the first time there was a keyboard instrument with a complete range of dynamics, from **very soft** to **very loud;** *legato, stacatto* and *sfortzando* at the fingertips of the player.

A Piano consists of a set of strings on a frame, an action to operate the hammers and dampers, and a soundboard to amplify the sound. Important features of Christofori's piano were:

(i) The **release mechanism** which allowed the hammer to drop back from the string even while the player's finger was on the key. This allowed the string to vibrate freely and the sound to be sustained.

(ii) The **loudness** of a note was perfectly controlled by the player's touch.

(iii) The **damper-action** was linked with the hammer action. The dampers normally rested on the strings but when a key was pressed a damper pad was raised, allowing the string to sound. The damper pad remained off the string as long as the key was held down. The damper pedal **(sustaining pedal)** raised the entire set of damper pads.

(iv) The **'soft pedal'** worked by moving the action sideways . . . the result was that each hammer struck only one string instead of three. (On upright pianos the soft pedal movs the hammers closer to the strings so that they strike with less force). On some pianos the soft pedal simply pushes a strip of felt between the hammers and the strings to muffle the sound.

Piano Action

1 — *hammer*
2 — *release mechanism*
3 — *string*
4 — *damper action*

key

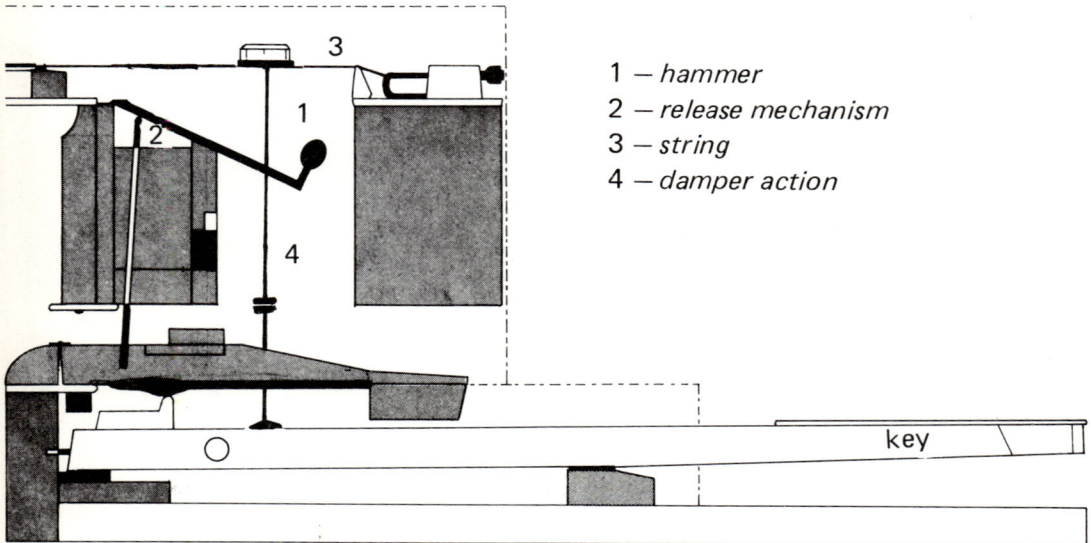

By 1825 Boston piano makers had developed an **iron frame.** This was a great improvement on the wooden frames previously used, which tended to warp and crack and slip out of tune easily. The iron frame allowed **longer** and **tighter stringing.** This increased the sound and improved the tone quality. It also made possible the nine foot long **Concert Grands** which could fill the biggest concert halls with sound.

Prominant piano manufacturers include: Steinway (U.S.); Bechstein (Germany); Broadwood (England); Petrov (Russia); Bluthner (France); Yahama (Japan).

9 —Musical Forms

FORM

Form means the overall plan or design of a piece of music. The phrases of a short piece of music will balance each other in a definite pattern. **Song and dance tunes** are often built on two ideas *(phrase A* and *phrase B),* which may be combined in several ways.

1. Binary form | A | B | or | A | A | B | B |

2. Ternary form | A | A | B | A | or | A | B | B | A | or | A | B | A | A |

In short **song tunes** each phrase has **four bars. Two** phrases make a **complete sentence** ending with a **cadence.** Most songs have **four phrases.**

Examples:

Baby Brother	**A A B B**
Flowers in the Valley	**A A B A**
Wi' a Hundred Pipers	**A A B B**
Bonnie Charlie	**A A B A**
Let Erin Remember	**A A B B**
The Wraggle Taggle Gipsies	**A B**

Dance Forms

The **court dances** of Medieval Europe found a permanent place in the music of the **Dance Suite** and the **Symphony.** Court dances were **restrained** and **dignified,** just like the starched costumes and stiff manners of that time. **Folk dances,** on the other hand, tended to be **lively** and **carefree.** Some of them were danced in a more genteel form by the courtiers, *e.g.* the *Gigue* and the *Hornpipe.* Some dances which are found in musical compositions are listed here:

188

I.C. Musicianship

Dance	Origin	Time	Character
Pavan	Italy	4/4	A slow, stately processional dance.
Sarabande	Spain	3/4	Begins on the first beat of the bar. A sober and steady dance.
Allemande	Germany	4/4	Moderate tempe, with flowing quavers and semiquavers.
Minuet	France	3/4	Three steady beats in the bar, begins on the downbeat. Danced very politely.
Courante	France	3/4	Running passages of music. Danced on the toes, with bowing and courtesies.
Gavotte	France	2/2	Starts on the third beat. Brisk tempo.
Bouree	France	4/4	Like the Gavotte, but starts on the fourth beat and is faster.
Gigue	England	6/8	Very fast and energetic.

The Dance Suite

The need for large-scale musical forms arose in the 16th century when instruments improved. Players looked for interesting pieces of music, longer than the song and dance tunes they were already using. At first, composers combined several dance tunes to make up one long piece. A group of five or six dances was called a **Suite.** The dances were usually in the same key but they differed in time and tempo. The basic dances in a suite were:

Allemande - Courante - Sarabande - Gigue

A *Gavotte, Bouree* or *Minuet* might be included before the *Gigue.* Bach wrote many dance suites and his *Suite for Orchestra in D* is based on that form.

Minuet and Trio

In European courts, up to the 18th century, the *Minuet* was the most popular dance. Because of its popularity it is often found in dance suites. Most symphonies, up to Beethoven's time, had a *Minuet* and *Trio* for the third movement. The *Trio* was a second *Minuet* to be played by a small group of instruments *(Trio = three).* The style is more flowing than the *Minuet* proper and sometimes the instruments imitate the droning of the bagpipes, *(e.g. Symphony in C* by Bizet). This is a reminder that the *Minuet* was a **country dance** before it was adopted by the court. The *Minuet* is always repeated in full after the *Trio,* making this a **Ternary Form.**

Fugue

A Fugue consists of a piece in **counterpoint,** for two or more voices, based on one main theme (called the **subject).** The subject is begun by one voice. The other voices enter in turn until all voices are singing together, but each is at a different part of the subject. The fugue is the most difficult kind of music to compose and it likewise offers the greatest challenge to the listener. Stripped of melody, a simple fugue might begin as follows

(cf. notes on Bach's *Suite in D, Unit 2).*

Sonata form

This form was developed by pre-classical composers, around 1700. Music is most intellectual in both Sonata Form and Fugue. Sonata Form uses **two themes (subjects),** which are worked out according to set rules.

Example from a sonata in C major

EXPOSITION
- (a) First subject is introduced in *key C.* It is a lively masculine tune.
- (b) Bridge passage modulating to *key G.*
- (c) Second subject in *key G* (or *A min*). It is lyrical and feminine in character.
- (d) Conclusion of exposition.

DEVELOPMENT
- (a) Both subjects are given a variety of treatments through key changes and different harmonisation.
- (b) Modulation to *key C* at conclusion.

RECAPITULATION
- (a) A repeat of the exposition section, but now the second subject is played in *key C* (the title key).
- (b) The first subject or a **Coda** rounds off the movement.

The divisions between the three sections are clearly marked by **bridge passages** or by **perfect cadences.** This form has attracted the most attention from composers. Numerous examples will be found in the Sonatas, Symphonies and Concertos of Haydn and Mozart. Later composers modify the rules to suit their own inspiration.

The Sonata and the Symphony

These are very large-scale works only part of which may be in Sonata Form, as described above. **A Sonata is a long work for solo instrument.** It has **three movements.** Usually only the first is in strict Sonata Form. **A Symphony** is similar in structure, but it **is for orchestra and has four movements.** There must be a feeling of **continuity** through the movements of a Symphony or Sonata; therefore people do not applaud until the end of the work, even though there is a short break between the movements. The movements are planned as follows:

First movement	In Sonata Form.
Second movement	Slow in tempo. Lyrical and easy to listen to, it is a release from the concentration required for the first movement.
Third movement	A dance form or a **Scherzo**, (*cf Minuet and Trio*)
Fourth movement	Sometimes in Sonata Form, often a **Rondo**. It is always lively and brings the music to an exciting conclusion.

The **Concerto** is another branch of sonata writing. It is **for solo instrument with full orchestral backing.** Pride of place is given to the **soloist,** especially in the **cadenza,** to allow him to show his skill and the capabilities of his instrument.

The **Tone Poem** or **Symphonic Poem** is **a single-movement Symphony,** favoured by Liszt and Strauss. As the name suggests, it is **music with a story** (Programme music). The **leading motive (leitmotif),** associated with Wagner is important in this form. It is a theme of special significance which recurs throughout the work.

Theme and Variations

The theme is stated in short simple form. Then the composer shows his inventiveness by presenting the theme in a variety of ways. In the *Trout Variations,* the theme is always clearly heard, while in Elgar's it is changed so much that it is very difficult to recognise it at times. In the past, **improvisation** was a skill which every keyboard player practised. It was usual at a recital for a performer to be given a theme on which he would improvise without preparation. Bach and Mozart could improvise for hours with amazing variations and development of a theme. In the Theme and Variation Form the composer uses techniques like those of the performer. Techniques for varying a theme include:

(a) Repeating it in different keys.
(b) Changing it from *major* to *minor,* or the reverse.
(c) Adding ornaments to the melody.
(d) Altering the note values (doubling or halving their values).
(e) Adding a countermelody to the theme.
(f) Changing the time signature.

Examples: **Haydn** *The 'Surprise' Symphony*
Elgar *The Enigma Variations*
Brahms *Variations on a Theme by Paganini*
Bach *Goldberg Variations*

Opera

An opera is **a play set to music.** The first true opera was Monteverdi's *Orfeo,* staged in Mantua in 1607. The stage play in **Italian opera** is just an 'excuse' for a feast of song, dance and spectacular entertainment. **The characters and the plot need not be true to life, the focal point is the voice of the singer.** Vocal **cadenzas** show the beauty and range of the trained voice. Early opera houses were built to stage ambitious scenes — burning cities, flying angels and dramatic illusions were possible.

German opera (music-drama), lorded over by Wagner, places more importance on the **dramatic plot** and **the characters. Arias** of regular form are little used; they are artificial and would delay the action. Instead, **the music moves as the plot demands.** In present time, music is used in movie films for similar reasons. The sound track carries forward the action and provides atmosphere; the music may be as important as the actors.

In terms of social history, the opera is interesting as one of the few occasions when class barriers were lowered. From the start, rich and poor alike shared the same auditorium, to enjoy the magical experience of opera.

Opera was and still is the music form that has something for everyone. Apart from the **Grand Opera** mentioned above, there is the **Light Opera** of Gilbert and Sullivan. *The Pirates of Penzance; Patience; The Mikado; etc.,* have been the staple fare of the English speaking public for over a century. **Operettas** like *The Student Prince; The Merry Widow* and **Broadway spectaculars** like *Oklahoma* and *West Side Story* continue to draw the crowds into the exciting world of the opera house.

A list of favourite operas would include:

Mozart *Don Giovanni; Marriage of Figaro; Magic Flute*
Donizetti *Lucia di Lammermoor*
Rossini *Barber of Seville*
Balfe *The Bohemian Girl*
Wallace *Maritana*
Gounod *Faust*
Verdi *Aida; Rigoletto; La Traviata*
Puccini *La Boheme; Madam Butterfly*
Bizet *Carmen*

Oratorio

This consists of a long dramatic work for **soloists, chorus** and **orchestra** based on a **Biblical** text. It is presented without scenery or costumes.

Examples: cf. Bach, Handel, Haydn, Elgar and Mendelssohn.

A scene from Bizet's famous opera "Carmen".

Overture

Originally a prelude to something bigger, the overture became a form in its own right early in the 19th century. It is now acceptable as an independent concert item.

Examples: **Beethoven** *Egmont Overture*
Brahms *Academic Festival Overture*
Rossini *William Tell Overture*
Tchaikovsky *1812 Overture*
Schubert *Rosamunde Overture*
Mendelssohn *Hebrides Overture; Italian Overture*

Rondo

A main theme alternates with any number of contrasting themes on the plan:-
A-B-A-C-A etc.
The piece must end with the main theme. The last movement of a Concerto is often in Rondo form.

Examples: **Haydn** *Trumpet Concerto* (last movement)
Mozart *Rondo à la Turk* (Piano sonata in *A min.*)
Eine Kleine Nachtmusik (last movement)

Exercise

Explain the following terms:

(a) Sonata form	(f) Fugue
(b) Rondo	(g) Variations
(c) Dance Suite	(h) Minuet and Trio
(d) Binary form	(i) Overture
(e) Opera	(j) Oratorio .

10 —Notation and Theory

THE STAVE

Musical sounds are written on a group of five lines called a **Stave** or **Staff.** Each line and space represents a certain pitch which is named by one of the letters- **A,B,C,D,E,F,G. Clef Signs** determine the naming of the lines and spaces, *e.g.*

The Treble (or G) sign shows where the **G line** is

The Bass (or F) sign shows where the **F line** is

The C sign shows where **Middle C** is

The treble and bass clefs are the ones most used and the diagram below shows how the musical symbols relate to a keyboard:

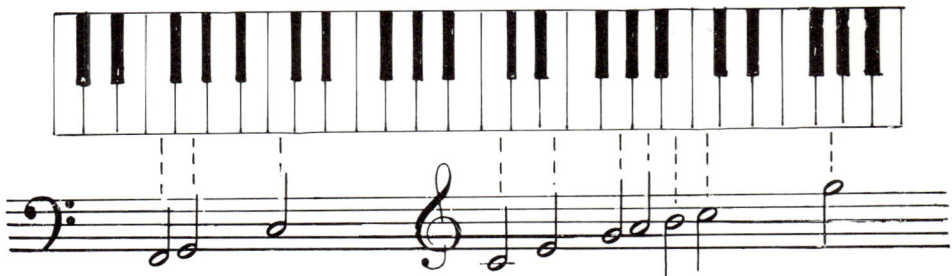

Note values

Note symbols have a **time-value** *i.e.* they show the duration of a note. The table below shows the most commom ones and their corresponding rests:

Table of Note Values			
Symbol	*Name*	*Rest*	*Time-Value in Units*
𝅝	semibreve	▬	1
𝅗𝅥	minim	▬	$\frac{1}{2}$
𝅘𝅥	crochet	𝄽	$\frac{1}{4}$
𝅘𝅥𝅮	quaver	𝄾	$\frac{1}{8}$
𝅘𝅥𝅯	semiquaver	𝄿	$\frac{1}{16}$
Dotted note: A dot after a note increases its duration by **half** of its value.			𝅗𝅥. = 𝅗𝅥 + 𝅘𝅥 𝅘𝅥. = 𝅘𝅥 + 𝅘𝅥𝅮

Time Signature

The **top number** tells how many **beats** are in each bar.
The **lower number** tells the **time-value** of each beat.

$\frac{2}{4}$	=	**Two** *crotchet* beats	in each bar
$\frac{2}{2}$	=	**Two** *minim* beats	in each bar
$\frac{3}{8}$	=	**Three** *quaver* beats	in each bar

Other terms:

Duple Time	means **two** beats of *any time-value* in a bar *e.g.* $\frac{2}{4}$ $\frac{2}{2}$
Triple Time	means **three** beats of *any time-value* in a bar *e.g.* $\frac{3}{4}$ $\frac{3}{8}$
Quadruple Time	means **four** beats of *any time-value* in a bar *e.g.* $\frac{4}{4}$
Compound Time	means **two or more triple** beats of *any time-value* in a bar *e.g.* $\frac{6}{8}$ $\frac{9}{8}$

SCALES

The scales most frequently used are the **Diatonic** *major* and *minor*.

Definitions:

    (i) The interval of a **semitone** is the smallest difference in pitch used in European music.

    (ii) A **tone** is an interval (difference) of two semitones.

    (iii) A **diatonic scale** is made up of both tones and semitones.

A musical scale is a series of notes in some special order, *e.g.* the *Major* scale:

TONE — TONE — SEMITONE: TONE: TONE — TONE — SEMITONE

TONIC	SUPERTONIC	MEDIANT	SUB DOMINANT	DOMINANT	SUB MEDIANT	LEADING NOTE	TONIC
I	II	III	IV	V	VI	VII	

Because the *major* scale is made up from two smaller scales, separated by a tone, some notes are more important than others. The **tonic, dominant** and **subdominant** are called **Primary Notes** because of their importance.

    A keyboard is arranged so that a *major* scale is available on the **white notes,** starting from **C.** The **black notes** show the positions of the other semitones.

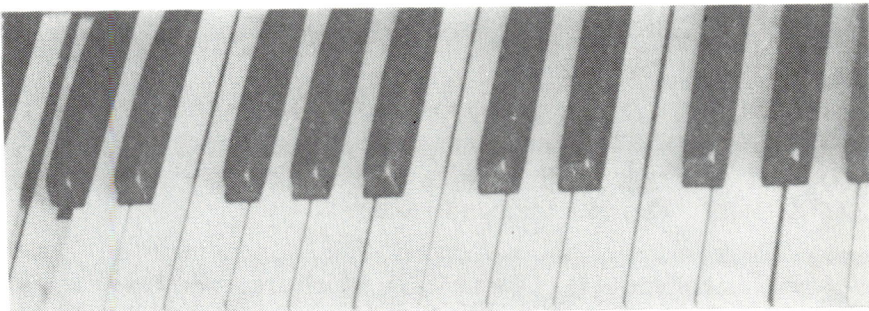

The Minor Scales

The minor scales are derived from the **Aeolion Mode** (**A to A** on the keyboard)
Because of this, some notes are altered by **accidentals** and not by a key-signature.

Modes

A **mode** is one of the many scales used in ancient music. Commonly used modes
were, the **Aeolian (A to A),** and the **Mixolydian (G to G). Plainsong** is modal and
sometimes Folksong. Modern musicians have begun to use modes again.

Intervals

An **interval** measures the distance in **pitch** separating two notes. To name an interval
each note is counted, as well as the steps in between.

Intervals of a 2nd, 5th, 8ve, and 9th:

C - D =2nd   **C(DEFGAB)C** = 8ve.
C(DEF)G =5th   **C(DEFGABC)D** = 9th.

Because the intervals of the scale include tones and semitones, some further description is necessary if one is to describe accurately the sound that is heard.

Although [music notation] and [music notation] are fifths, each does not represent equal differences of pitch. When the first chord is struck on the keyboard, the effect is completely harmonious. This fifth (tonic to dominant) is called a **perfect** fifth. The other fifth is somewhat discordant — it is not a perfect fifth.

Perfect Intervals: The 4th, 5th and 8ve in a major scale are called perfect intervals.

Major Intervals: The other intervals from the *tonic* of a major scale are called major intervals.

Minor Intervals: A minor interval is a *semitone less* than a major interval.

Examples:

MAJOR

MINOR

The Three-Note Chord

The basic unit of harmony is the Three-Note Chord **(triad).** It is formed by placing a third and a fifth above any note.

The note on which a triad is built is called the **Root.** The **lowest** note in a chord is called the **Bass.** Note that the root is not *always* the bass.

Root	G	G	G
Bass	G	B	D

A Triad is named after the degree of the scale on which it is built.

C major

I II III IV V

A Triad is *major* when the **third above the root** is major.

A Triad is *minor* when the **third above the root** is minor.

Tonic, Dominant and **Subdominant** are ·called **Primary Triads.** The **major, minor** and **perfect** intervals are **consonant** *i.e.* they sound satisfactory and complete. Others are **dissonant** *e.g.* the leading note Triad (VII).

MUSIC TO WORDS

Rhythm Patterns

The building block of rhythm is the **foot. A foot (musical or poetic) is an arrangement of strong and weak pulses.** A musical foot differs from the poetic foot in being a matter of **strict time.** Compare the following:

There are many possible rhythm patterns for this line. Some would be more suitable
than others. The second example, for instance, is less suitable than the first. The following are some guidelines for writing a rhythm pattern to verse:

1. Decide on a suitable tempo.
2. Read the line aloud to find the accented syllables. Mark each syllable and
   draw bar-lines before each **strong** accent.
3. Decide on the note-value of each syllable and set a time signature.
4. Check that each bar is complete in time values, and that *every* syllable has a
   corresponding note.

Composing a melody

A melody is an ordered series of notes making a complete musical sentence.
The ear is the best judge of what makes a good melody, but to begin melody writing
some rules should be observed:

1. The notes move by step mainly.
2. Leaps are confined to notes of the tonic and dominant triads.
3. A melody should end on the tonic, making a **perfect cadence.**
4. A less complete cadence could occur midway through the melody. It is made
   by ending the phrase on the dominant **(imperfect cadence).**
5. The opening phrase is balanced in some way by the answering phrase. Both
   phrases should be the same length and have some rhythmic and melodic
   contrast.

More can be learned about what makes a good melody by singing and listening to examples from the song section. Several examples of the above rules are found in the
following simple, but good, melody:

Cadences

Cadences are the punctuation marks of music. A cadence has two parts: the
preparatory chord and the *final chord.* To sound complete a piece should end with a
perfect cadence. The **plagal cadence** is another form used to bring a piece to a
close. It s found most often in Church music. The **interrupted cadence** is less
definite than the **imperfect.** As a rule, to express these cadences, a melody will approach its **final note** with a note of the **preparatory chord.**

Perfect cadence (V–I)

V   –   I

Plagal Cadence (IV–I)

IV   –   I

Imperfect cadence (I,IV *or* VI–V)

I   (IV or VI)   – V

Interrupted Cadence (V–VI).

V   –   VI

Key Relationship

Key or **tonality** means that the notes of a particular piece of music have a special relationship with each other, *e.g.* they all belong to the **same scale.**

The keys that have most notes in common are said to be 'closely related'. **C** and **G** have six notes in common, while **C** and **D** have only five. Therefore **C** is more closely related to **G** than to **D.**

When one compares the triads that are common to two keys, the idea of key-relationship becomes more evident. **C** and **G** have four triads in common, **C** and **D** have only two, while **C** and **A** have none.

The closeness or remoteness of keys is indicated by their key-signatures, the number of **accidentals** in the signature is the clue. **A** (♯♯♯), is close to **E** (♯♯♯♯). **A** is also close to **D** (♯♯); but **E** (♯♯♯♯) is more remote from **D** (♯♯). The following diagram shows the degrees to which keys are related:

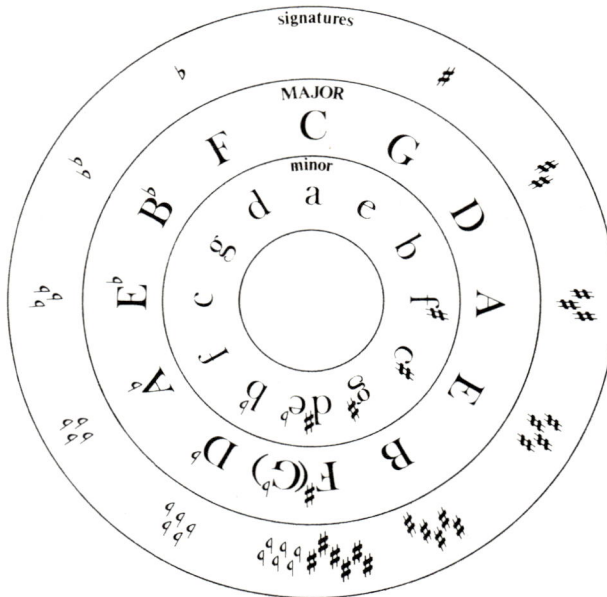

If a piece of music remained in the same key all the time, using only the harmonies of that key, it would probably be a monotonous piece of music. Music usually moves into other keys, and returns to the original key at the end. This makes for variety and contrast. A temporary change of key is described as **Modulating.** The shortest possible modulation is a **Transition.**

To make a Transition in a Melody

A transition uses only **two** notes of the new key. These are often **leading notes** and **tonic.**

Method

1. Introduce the **leading note** of the new key (B below).
2. Follow with the **tonic** of the new key (C).

If the leading note of the new key is **not** a note of the old key (the **B** here does not belong to key **F**), the change of key is clearly heard.

When the piece is harmonised the entry of the new key is much more noticeable.

SYMBOLS AND TERMS

Symbols

Pause	⌢˙	_Pause on the note_
Sharp	♯	_Raises the note after it by a semitone._
Flat	♭	_Lowers the note after it by a semitone._
Natural	♮	_Cancels a previous sharp or flat._
Tie	⌢	_The two notes are held for their combined time-value._
Slur	⌒	_Shows a single phrase or where a breath is taken._
Crescendo	◁	_Becomes gradually louder._
Decrescendo	▷	_Becomes gradually softer._
Stacatto	˙♩	_The notes are played in a detached manner._
Legato	⌒	_The notes are joined together smoothly._
Ledger lines		_Extend the range of the five-line stave upwards or downwards._

Expression marks

p = **piano (soft)** f = **forte (loud)**.
m = **moderately**, _e.g._ mf = **moderately loud**.
sf = **sforzando (very strongly accented)**.

COMMONLY USED TERMS

Accelerando	gradually faster
Ad Lib.	as the player or singer wishes
Allargando	gradually slower to broaden out
Arco	use the bow (for string players)
A tempo	resume original speed (after a change of speed)
Cantabile	in a singing style
Capo	the beginning (*e.g. da capo* = from the beginning)
Con	with (*e.g. con sordini* = with mutes)
Diminuendo	gradually softer
Dolce	sweetly
Espressivo	with expression
Fine	the end
Giusto	strict (*e.g. tempo giusto* = in strict time)
Glissando	the effect got by drawing the fingers along the keys of a piano
Grazioso	gracefully
Ma non troppo	not too much (*Allegro ma non troppo* = not too fast)
Marcato	marked or accented
Meno mosso	less movement, slower
Ped.	pedal, use the sustaining pedal of the piano
Piu	more (*piu allegro* = more quickly)
Pizzicato	plucked (in string music)
Poco a poco	little by little
Rallentando	gradually slower (*Rall.*)
Ritardando	gradually slower (*Rit.*)
Rubato	not keeping strict time (as in Chopin's music)
Scherzando	in a playful manner
Senza	without (*senza sordini* = without mutes)
Sordini	mutes or soft pedal of piano
Sostenuto	sustained
Tutti	all
Un poco	a little

Exercise Material

Identify the following excerpts from the songs and orchestral scores on your course.

23

24

25

26

27

28

29

30

31

32

33

34

35

36

37

38

39

40

Identify each of the following instruments and say to which 'family' each belongs. Make a sketch of each of the instruments and write a brief note about each one.

APPENDIX

Suggestions for Aural Exercises

The resource material for the following questions should be prepared on tape (*cf. page 176* for some suggestions for extra-curricular examples). For some of the questions, prepared answer sheets may also be required. The question material is played four times, with a short interval between each playing. Usually, there is a longer interval before the final playing to allow students time to complete their answers. Some of the following terms may help students to make specific points in their answers — **mood; texture; rhythm; time; tempo; melodic shape; phrasing; major/minor; orchestration; homophonic; contrapunctual, classical, baroque; modern,**

1. **Resource Material:** Two short (30 sec.) excerpts from either
    - (a) a prescribed work and an unprescribed, or
    - (b) different sections of a single work.
    (The excerpts selected should be clearly either contrasting or similar in style.)

Questions.
- (i) List some points of difference/similarity between these two pieces.
- (ii) How would you describe the mood of each piece?

2. **Resource Material:** A short (60 sec.) excerpt from an unprescribed work, having clearly defined features of style or structure.

Questions
- (i) Write a programme note on this piece of music.
- (ii) Mention some ways in which it resembles a piece on your course.

3. **Resource Material:** A major theme from one of the prescribed works.

Questions
- (i) Name the composer of this piece from your course.
- (ii) What part does this theme play in the overall structure of the work?

4. **Resource Material:** Extract from Irish song and art song.

Questions
- (i) Point out some of the differences between the songs played.
- (ii) Name other songs on your course similar to the songs just played.
- (iii) Mention some of the points of similarity in each case.

5. **Resource Material:** 8/16 bars of melody sung or played on a solo instrument. Class sheets having the same piece incompletely notated.

Questions
(i) On the sheet supplied fill in bar lines, tempo mark and time signature.
(ii) Insert suitable expression marks.
(iii) Indicate phrasing with slurs.
(iv) Write in the missing notes or accidentals at the points indicated.

6. **Resource Material:** Short phrase, clearly played on solo instrument preceded by keynote.

Questions
(i) Write down the rhythm pattern of the phrase.
(ii) Write down the melody in any key you wish.

7. **Resource Material:** 8/16 bars from a Court or Folk dance.

Questions
(i) Write down the prevailing rhythm pattern of this dance.
(ii) Write down the time signature and a suitable tempo mark.
(iii) Is the dance played a Gavotte, Gigue, *etc?*
(iv) Name an Irish dance of similar character.

8. **Resource Material:** A short excerpt from a prescribed or unprescribed work (*cf. page 176)* which features a solo instrument, a duo, instrumental family or en-semble.

Questions
(i) Name the instrument or members of the instrumental group heard.
(ii) What other instrument(s) might suitably be used for this music?

9. **Resource Material:** Recording of an eight-bar phrase, clearly sung. Class sheets, giving words and melody for the first four bars, words only for the last (note values may be supplied).

Question
Write down the last four bars heard, or, supply your own answering phrase to the one given.

10. **Taped Projects:** Prepare and present on tape, with narrative and musical illus-trations, a radio programme on some of these topics:
    (i) The life story of Bach/Handel, *etc.*
    (ii) Irish music recorded by popular artists.
    (iii) Traditional Irish music.
    (iv) Anglo-Irish music.
    (v) Folk music/Religious Music/Art Song.

Index